31 SUBWAY
KEITH HARING
DRAWINGS

Distributed by
Princeton University Press, 41 William Street Princeton, New Jersey 08540

press.princeton.edu

nomorerulers.com

@nomorerulers

~~NO MORE RULERS~~

Cloth ISBN 9780691229973

Library of Congress Control Number: 2021933129

British Library Cataloging-in-Publication Data is available

This book has been composed in Helvetica Neue LT Pro

Printed on acid-free paper

Printed in China

Published in conjunction with the exhibition
Keith Haring: 1978–1982 at the Brooklyn Museum
March 16–July 8, 2012

31 SUBWAY KEITH HARING DRAWINGS

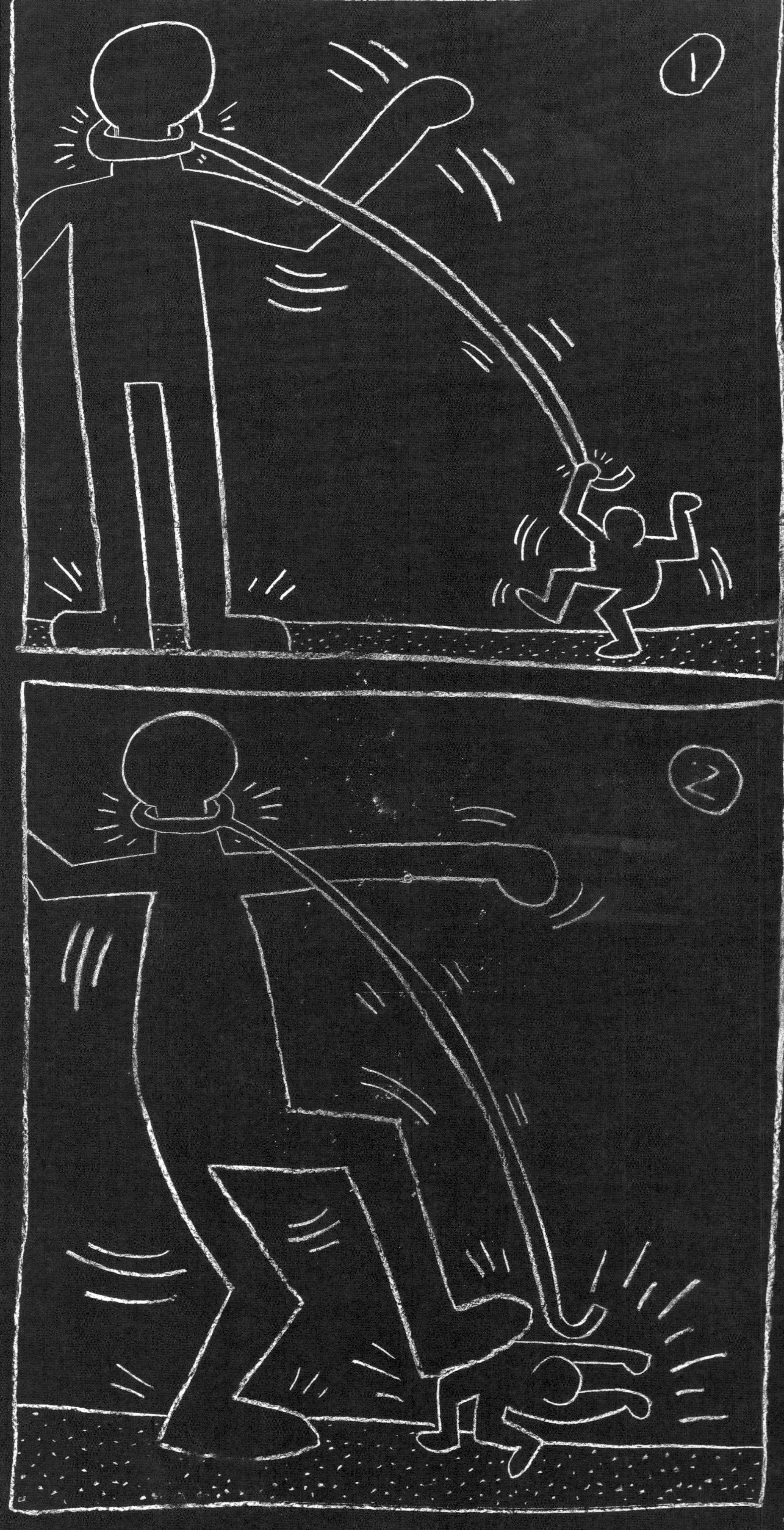

Foreword: Pulling from the Infinite Stream

Larry Warsh

I have only a hazy memory of my first encounter with a Keith Haring subway drawing. It would have been back in the early 1980s, probably in a downtown station: West Fourth Street in Greenwich Village, perhaps, or Delancey Street on the Lower East Side. I can't even recall which of his many iconic images — the radiant baby, the barking dog — it featured. But it didn't take long for me to realize how important these drawings were, not only in the evolution of Haring's work, but in the broader scope of contemporary art.

That, in a nutshell, is what collectors do: they recognize, with great clarity, that a given artwork or artist is — or more usually, will be — significant to the art and culture of their time. It's a given that as a society, we rarely make such judgements on the spot with any accuracy. But collectors, with their passion for discovery and confidence in their own tastes, sometimes have a knack for seeing ahead in this way.

When I became aware of Keith Haring's subway drawings as significant art of our time, I became, I think, that kind of collector. It was obvious to me that these works would be among his most important, and despite their ephemeral nature, his most enduring. I felt compelled to acquire them and went about assembling this collection, one by one, over the years. I was not a personal friend of Keith's — though we had our downtown-art-scene moments together — and I've since heard that he didn't like the idea of people owning the subway drawings. He felt they should have been left in place for all to enjoy, until fate and the MTA caused them to disappear under the next ad.

But that, too, is what collectors do: they pull, from the infinite stream of objects and images that cross their paths, those that speak to them for whatever reason, as the subway drawings spoke to me. These works have a natural energy and flow that still captivates me more than thirty years later. And I can appreciate the marks that attest to their origins on station walls: the rips and wrinkles that define their gleefully beat-up character. They're not perfect or pristine, and were never meant to be. It's key to their inception — the way they were made and how they connect to their audiences as public art. Haring always meant for this art to be accessible and comprehensible, and for everyone to think about and interpret the work for themselves. In the universe that he conjured up in the subway drawings, the sense of egalitarianism extends to all ages, including the very young.

In the essays that follow, Keith himself has the first word: the artist's statement that originally appeared in the book *Art in Transit: Subway Drawings*, published in 1984. The essay after it, by Henry Geldzahler, was the introduction to that book. The original version of Jeffrey Deitch's essay first appeared in *Keith Haring*, the catalogue for a show at Tony Shafrazi Gallery in 1982. It is personally satisfying to retrieve these texts, which speak so eloquently of Haring's art and of the era in which they first appeared. The essay by Carlo McCormick, written for this volume, insightfully recasts Haring's legacy in contemporary terms.

I am pleased and proud that these subway drawings are once again being shown to the public, as a grouping of works with their own coherence and logic. Seeing them now, decades after their underground creation, it is easy to identify them as crucial forebears to the current street art movement. At times I like to ponder what people will think of them a hundred years from now. Because I have every confidence that, pulled from the river of daily life and rescued from the fate that so many of the subway drawings met, these most fleeting of artistic expressions will, paradoxically, be there for the next century to enjoy. ■

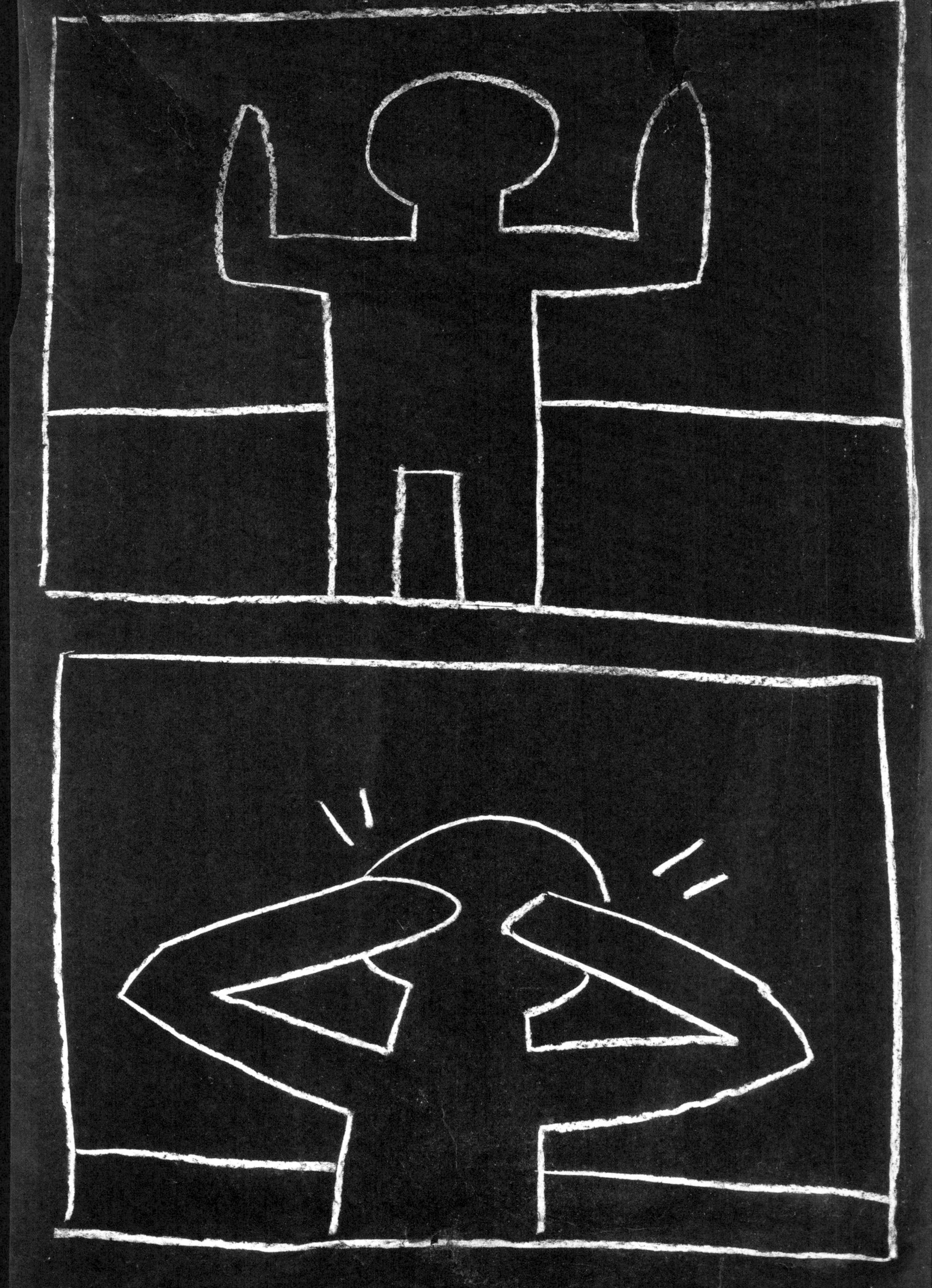

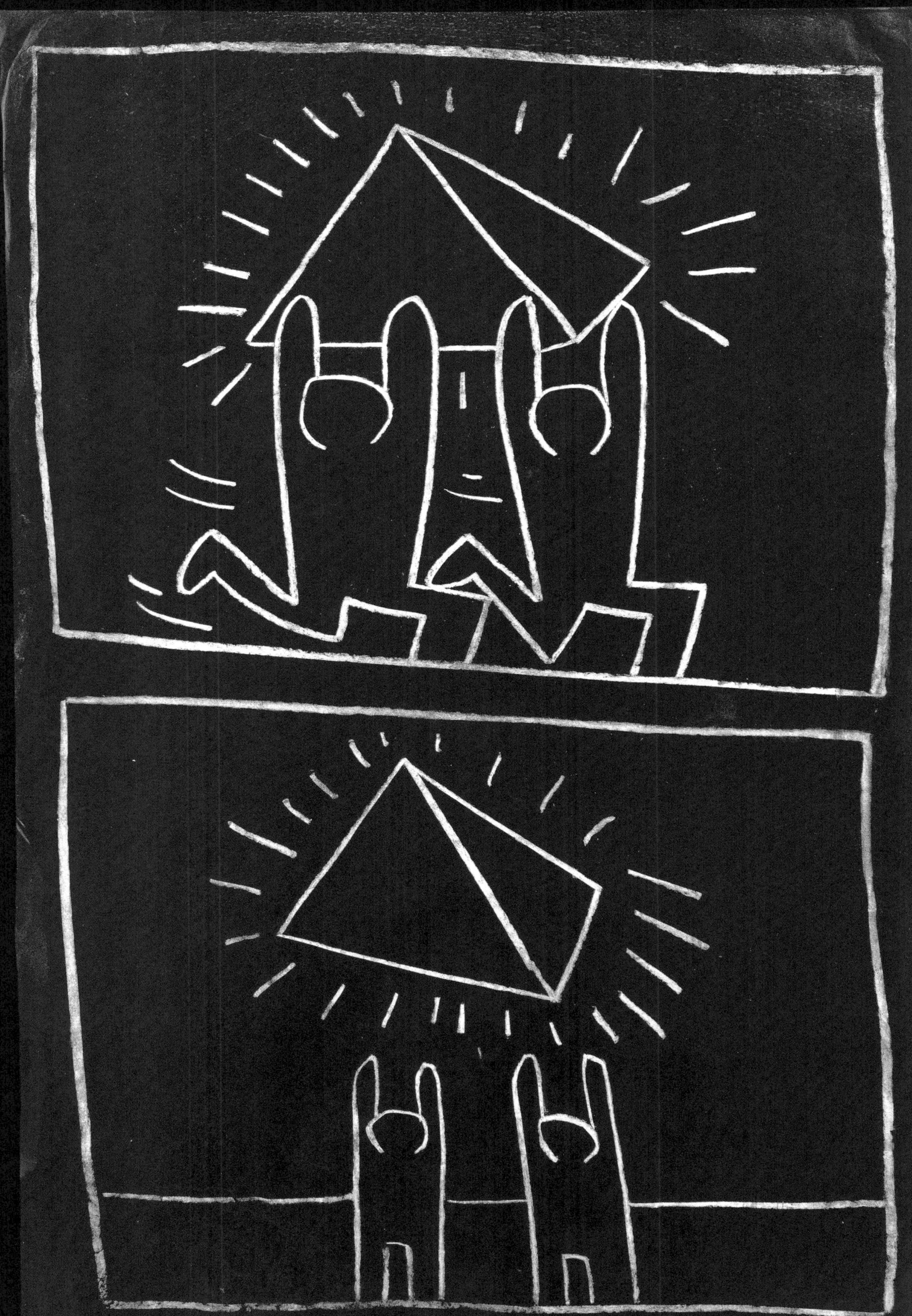

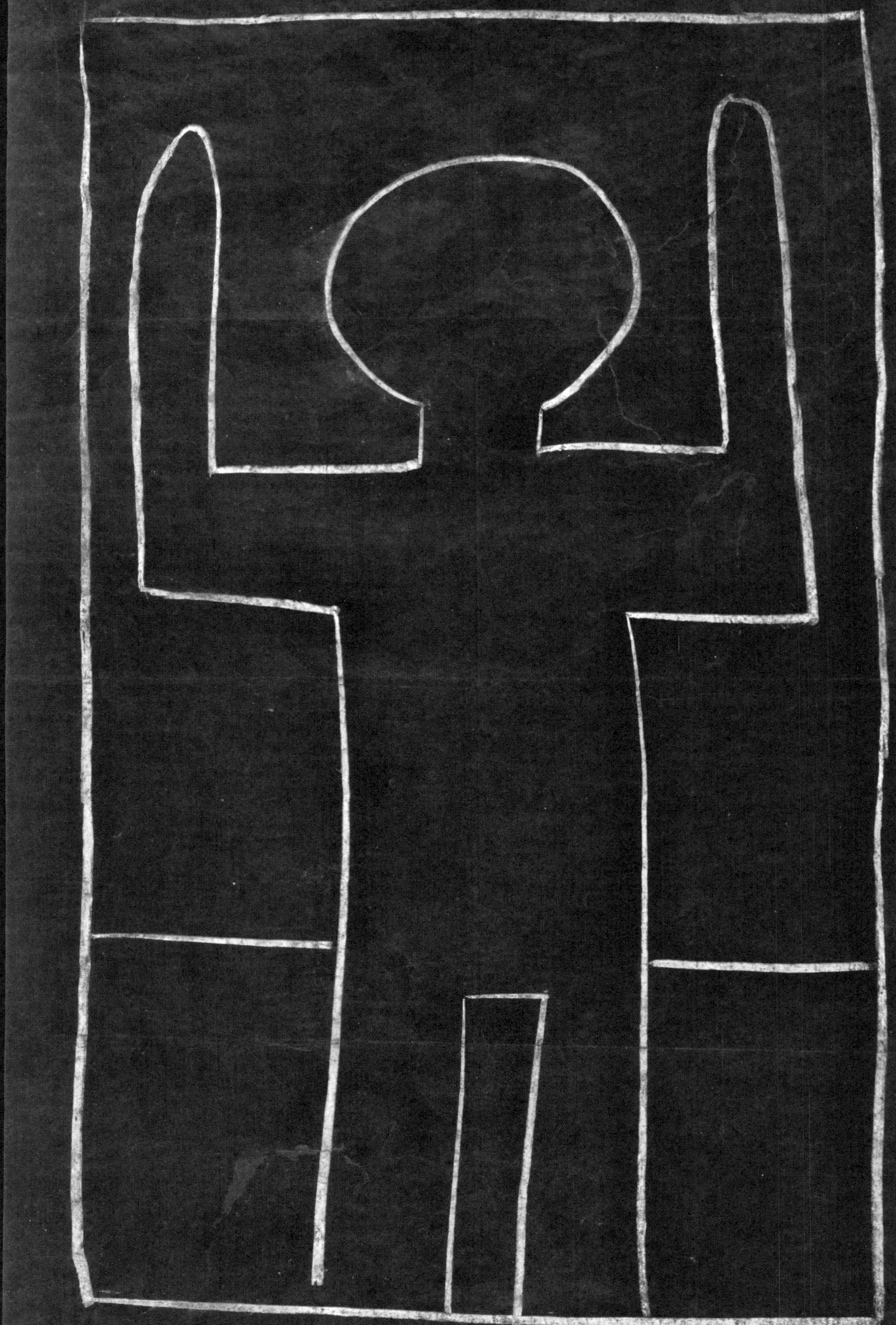

The Subway Is Still My Favorite Place to Draw

Keith Haring

I have been drawing since I was four years old. I learned to draw from my father, who would entertain me by inventing cartoon animals. Although he never pursued an artistic career, he encouraged me to continue drawing throughout my school years. Drawing became a way of commanding respect and communicating with people. When I was eighteen, my work, which had been primarily cartoon-oriented, became increasingly abstract and concerned with spontaneous action. I became interested in Eastern Calligraphy and the art of the Gesture. When I moved to New York City at the age of twenty, I started to experiment with drawing on paper that was so large that I had to stand inside the drawing. Although my work was still "Abstract" at this time, I became aware of the vast differences in people's responses to the work. Different people saw different things in the drawings. I remember most clearly an afternoon of drawing in a studio that had large doors that opened onto Twenty-second Street. All kinds of people would stop and look at the huge drawing and many were eager to comment on their feelings toward it. This was the first time I realized how many people could enjoy art if they were given the chance. These were not the people I saw in the museums or in the galleries but a cross-section of humanity that cut across all boundaries. This group of different people living and working together in harmony has always been my prime attraction to New York.

I arrived in New York at a time when the most beautiful paintings being shown in the city were on wheels — on trains — paintings that traveled to you instead of vice versa. I was immediately attracted to the subway graffiti on several levels: the obvious mastery of drawing and color, the scale, the pop imagery, the commitment to drawing worthy of risk and the direct relationship between artist and audience. I had no intention, however, of jumping on the bandwagon and imitating their style.

For two years, I was an observer. During that time, my art was going through several changes. I began making videotapes and doing performances. I was introduced to the work of William Burroughs and began experimenting with words and meaning in a similar style. I studied semiotics, the science of signs and symbols.

In 1980, I returned to drawing with a new commitment to purpose and reality. If I was going to draw, there had to be a reason. That reason, I decided, was for people. The only way art lives is through the experience of the observer. The reality of art begins in the eyes of the beholder and gains power through imagination, invention, and confrontation.

Doing things in public was not a new idea. The climate of art in New York at that time was certainly moving in that direction. It seemed obvious to me when I saw the first empty subway panel that this was the perfect situation. The advertisements that fill every subway platform are changed periodically. When there aren't enough new ads, a black paper panel is substituted. I remember noticing a panel in the Times Square station and immediately going aboveground and buying chalk. After the first drawing, things just fell into place. I began drawing in the subways as a hobby on my way to work. I had to ride the subways often and would do a drawing while waiting for a train. In a few weeks, I started to get responses from people who saw me doing it.

After a while, my subway drawings became more of a responsibility than a hobby. So many people wished me luck and told me to "keep it up" that it became difficult to stop. From the beginning, one of the main incentives was this contact with people. It became a rewarding experience to draw and to see the drawings being appreciated. The number of people passing one of these drawings in a week was phenomenal. Even if the drawing remained up for only one day, enough people saw it to make it easily worth my effort.

The panel remains from a few days to a few weeks before a new advertisement is posted on top of it. This constant replenishment forces me to keep inventing new images and ideas.

The images are part of the collective consciousness of modern man. Sometimes they stem from world events, sometimes from ideas about technology or people changing roles in relation to God and evolution. All of the drawings use images that universally "readable". They are often inspired by popular culture.

The drawings are designed to provoke people to think and use their own imagination. They don't have exact definitions but challenge the viewer to assert his or her own ideas and interpretation. Sometimes, people find this uncomfortable, especially because the drawings are in a space usually reserved for advertisements which tell you exactly what to think. Sometimes the advertisements on the side of the empty panels provide inspiration for the drawings and often create ironic associations.

When there are graffiti "tags" (signatures) on the black panel before I arrive, I usually draw around and in between the signatures. I would never draw over other people's tags. This mutual respect among graffiti writers, however, does not extend to other people. Sometimes other people sign my drawings after I've left. Sometimes they erase them, cross them out, or even steal them. These are the only things that inhibit my work in the subway.

The drawings are by necessity quick and simple. This is not only for easy readability but also to avoid getting arrested. Technically they are still graffiti. Because they are only chalk and the black ads are only temporary, it is hard to call them vandalism; however, different policeman respond in different ways. I have been caught many times. Some cops have given me a $10.00 ticket, some have handcuffed me and taken me in. By the time they let me go, most of them tell me they like the drawing, but they're just doing their job. More than once, I've been taken to a station handcuffed by a cop who realized, much to his dismay, that the other cops in the precinct were my fans and were anxious to meet me and shake my hand.

I have been drawing in the subway for three years now, and although my career aboveground has skyrocketed, the subway is still my favorite place to draw. There is something very "real" about the subway system and the people who travel in it; perhaps there is not another place in the world where people of such diverse appearance, background, and life-style have intermingled for a common purpose. In this underground environment, one can often feel a sense of oppression and struggle in the vast assortment of faces. It is in this context that an expression of hope and beauty carries the greatest rewards.

One month after I began drawing in the subway, my friend, Tseng Kwong Chi, began voluntarily to undertake the task of documenting these works. Usually after I finish a daily route I telephone Kwong Chi and explain the location of the new drawings. He then retraces my path and captures the drawings in their natural setting. Often the eye of the photographer reveals situations and coincidences that I wasn't even conscious of during my speedy performances. These photographs are all that remain from the thousands of drawings I've done in the last three years. And for that I am eternally grateful.

This book is a culmination of our combined efforts, along with our good friend Dan Friedman who helped pull the book together, and make it a reality. The text by Henry Geldzahler, a former Commissioner of Cultural Affairs for the City of New York, is wonderfully appropriate for this book.

Special thanks to Kurt Thometz, Alexander Agayan, Tony Shafrazi, and Juan DuBose, who each made important contributions.   ■

This essay was originally published in *Art in Transit: Subway Drawings* by Keith Haring; Photos by Tseng Kwong Chi; Introduction by Henry Geldzahler (Harmony Books, 1984). Reprinted with permission.

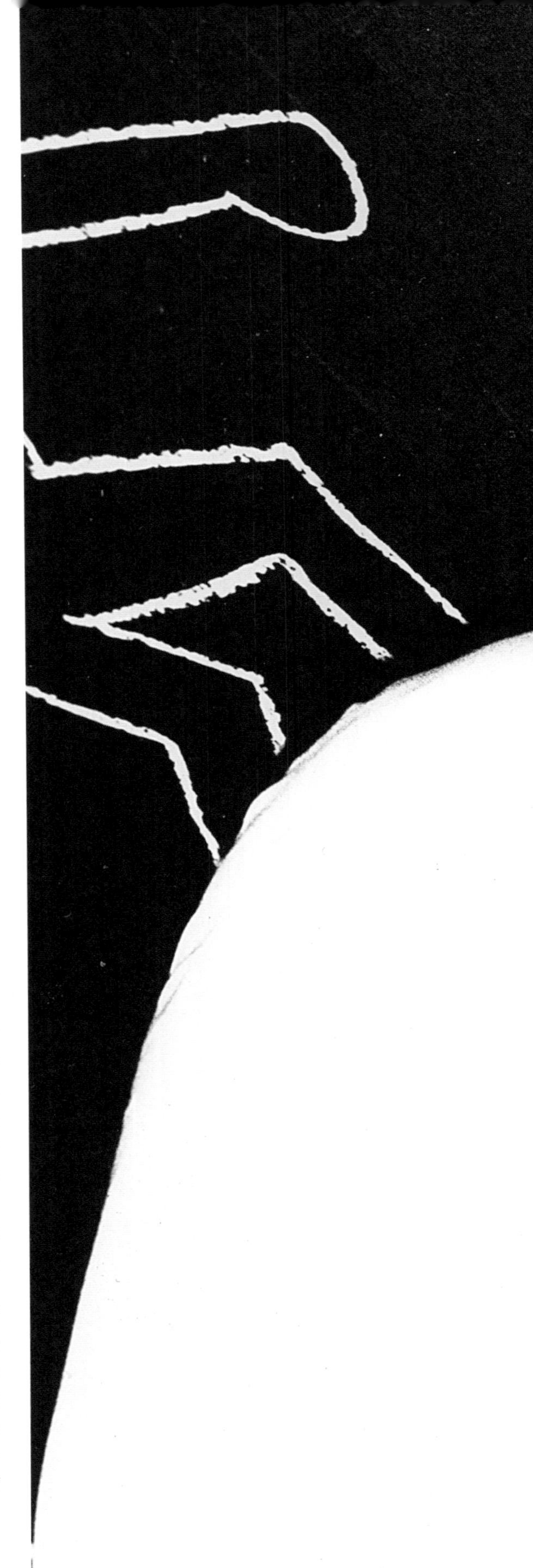

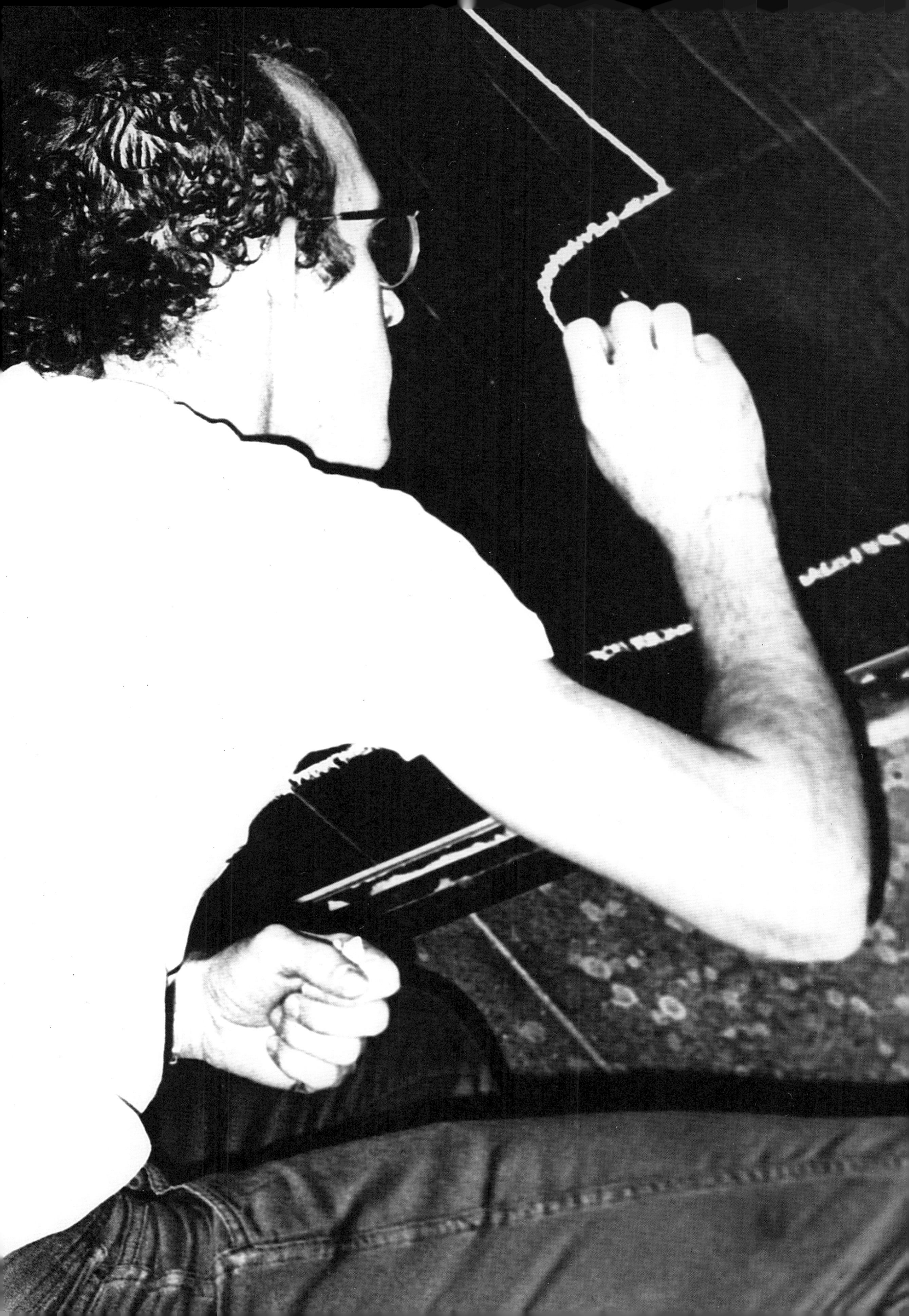

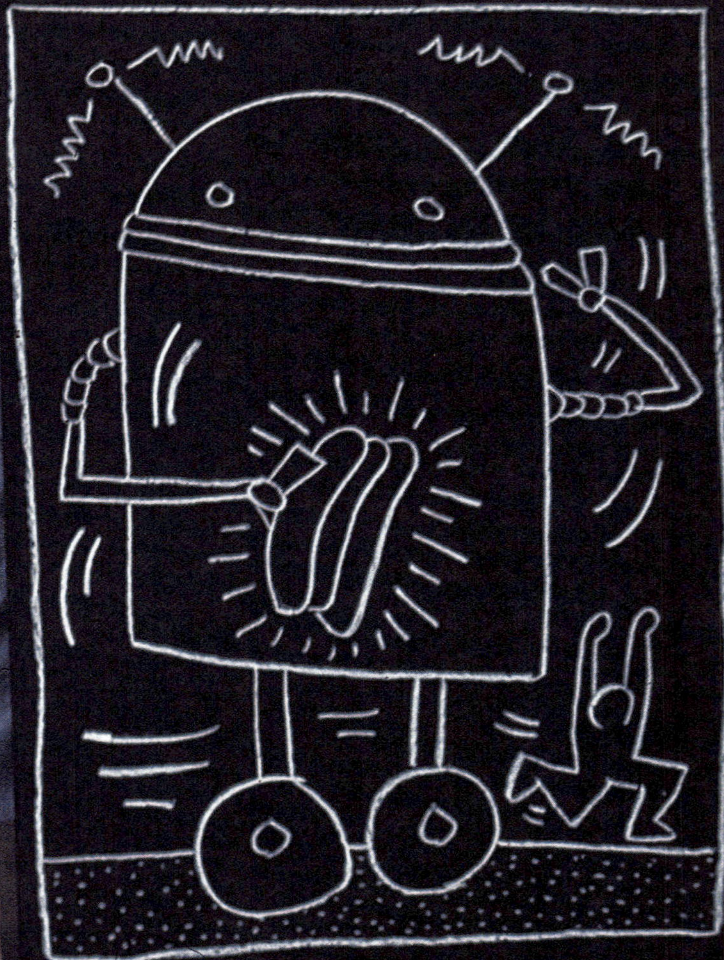
MUSEUM OF MODERN ART
ULD YOU BUY
HOT DOG
M THIS MAN?
Good in every way.

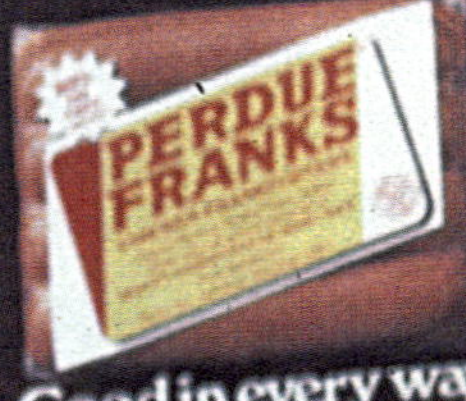
PERDUE
FRANKS

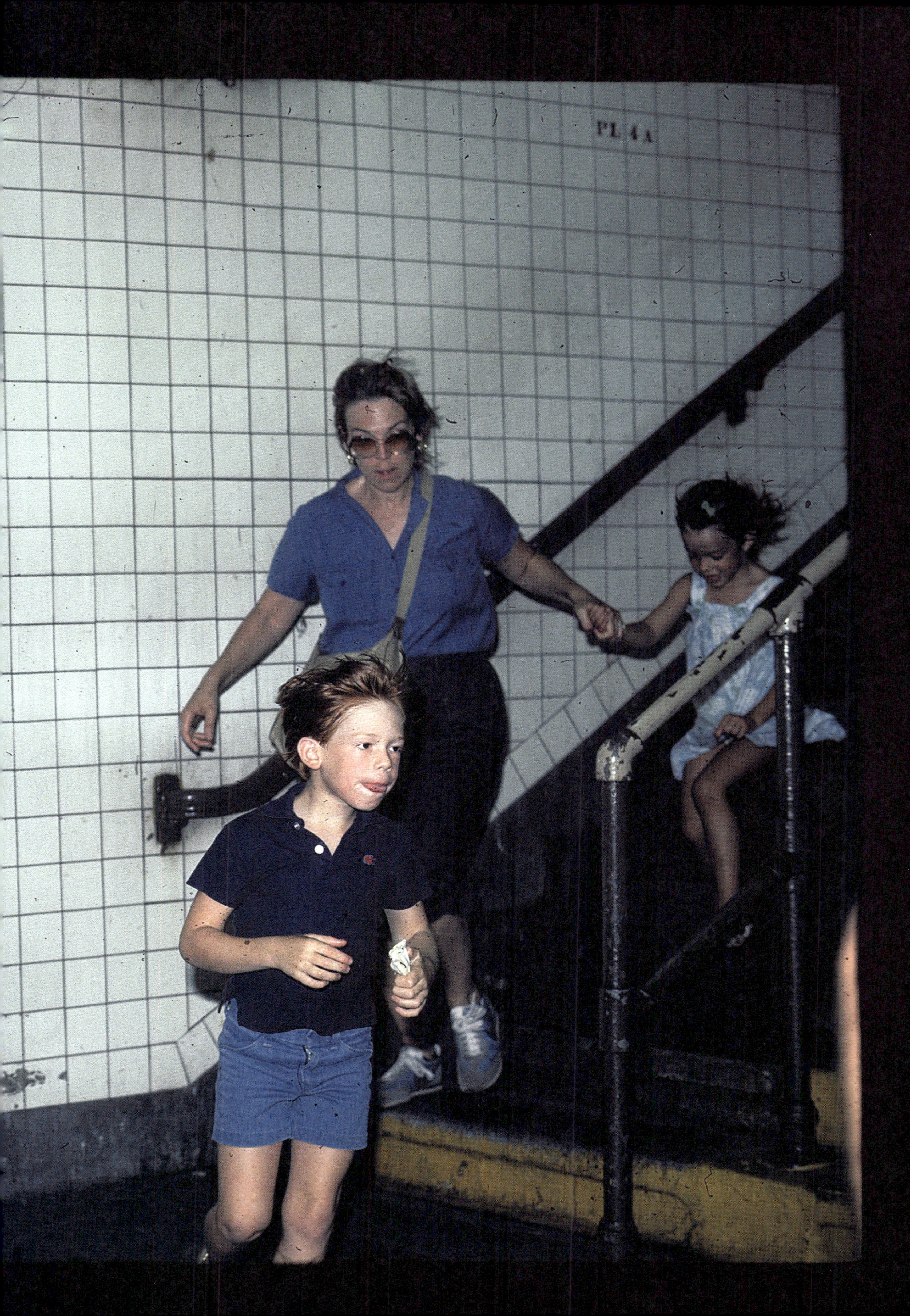
PL 4 A

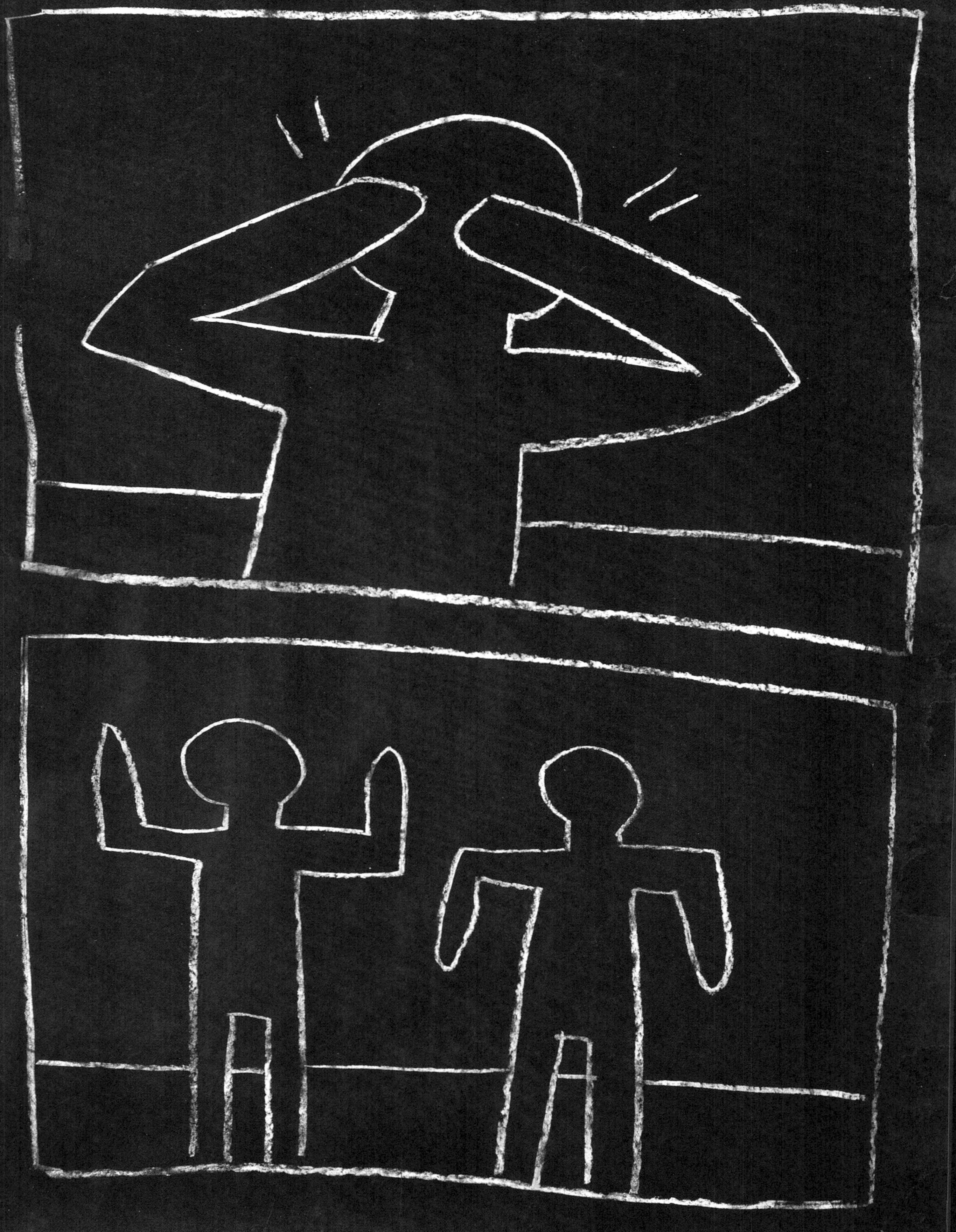

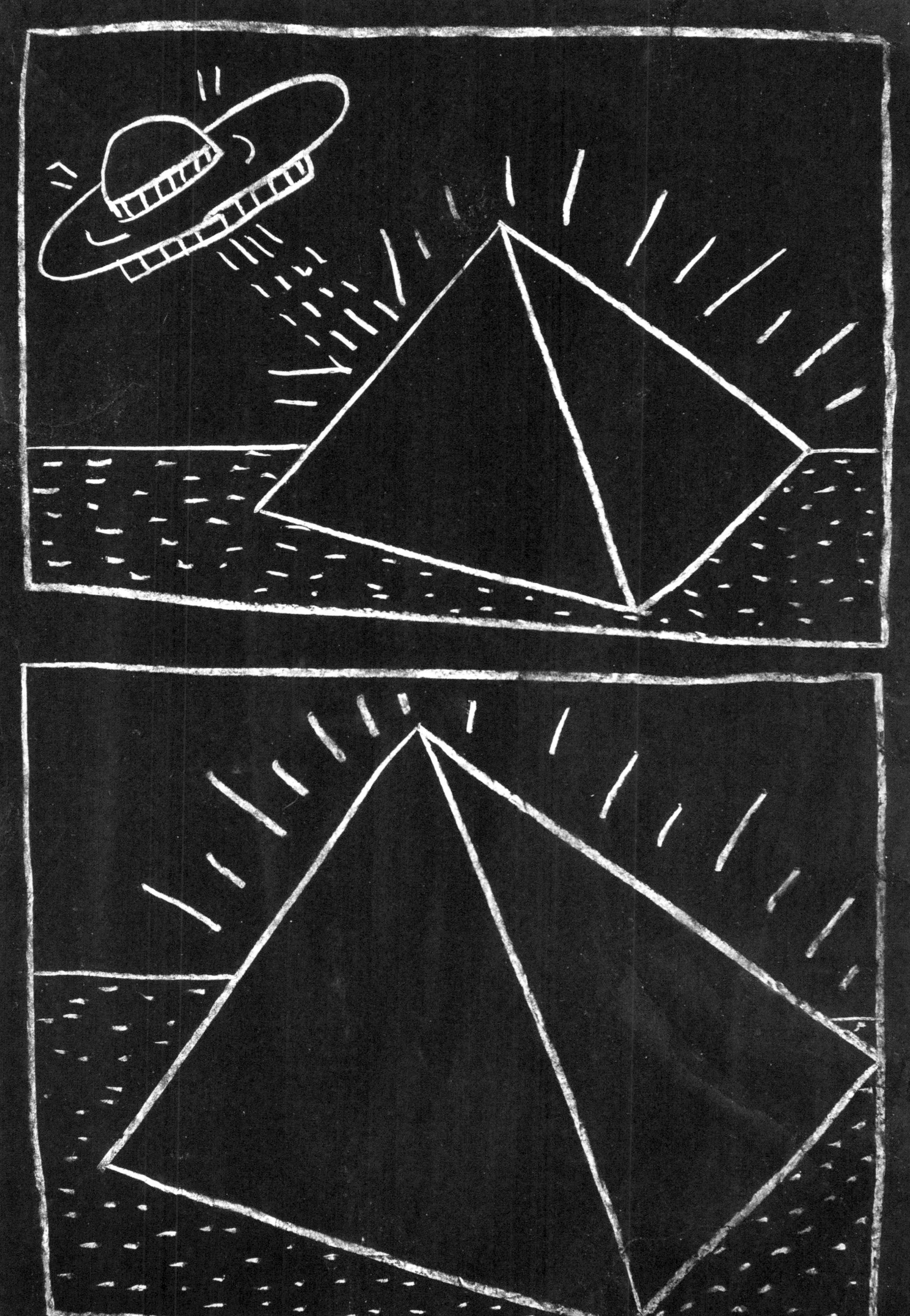

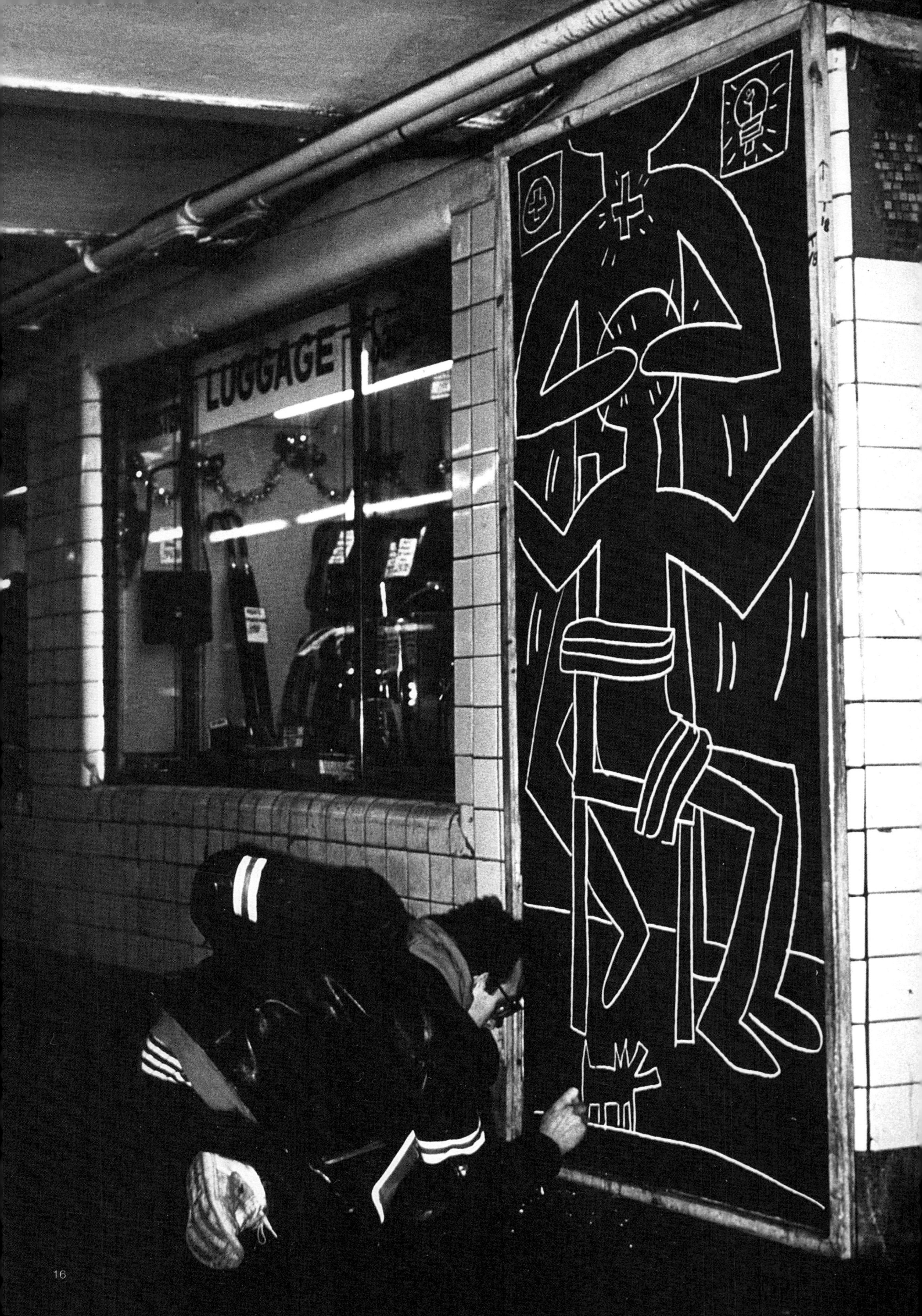
LUGGAGE

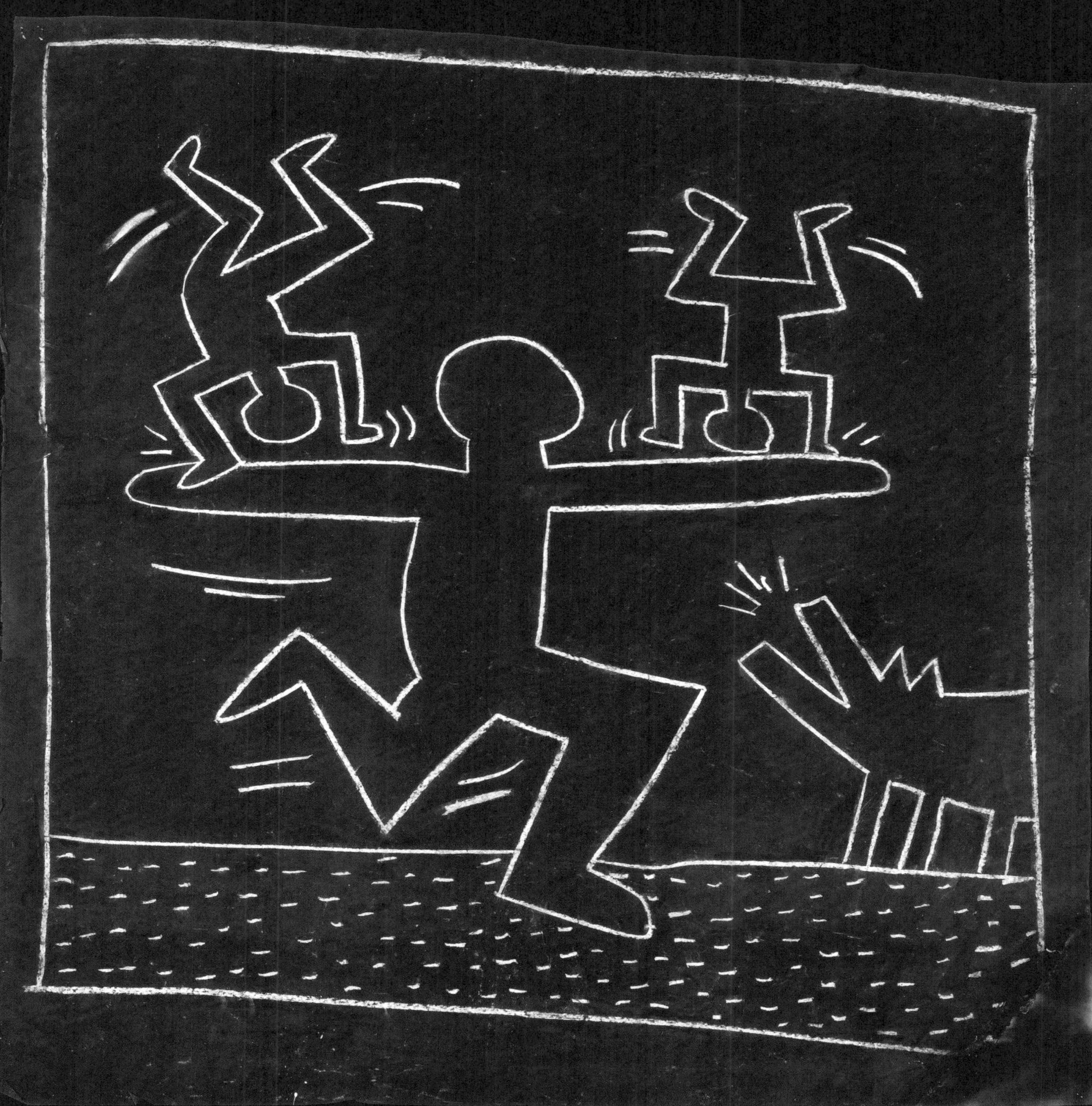

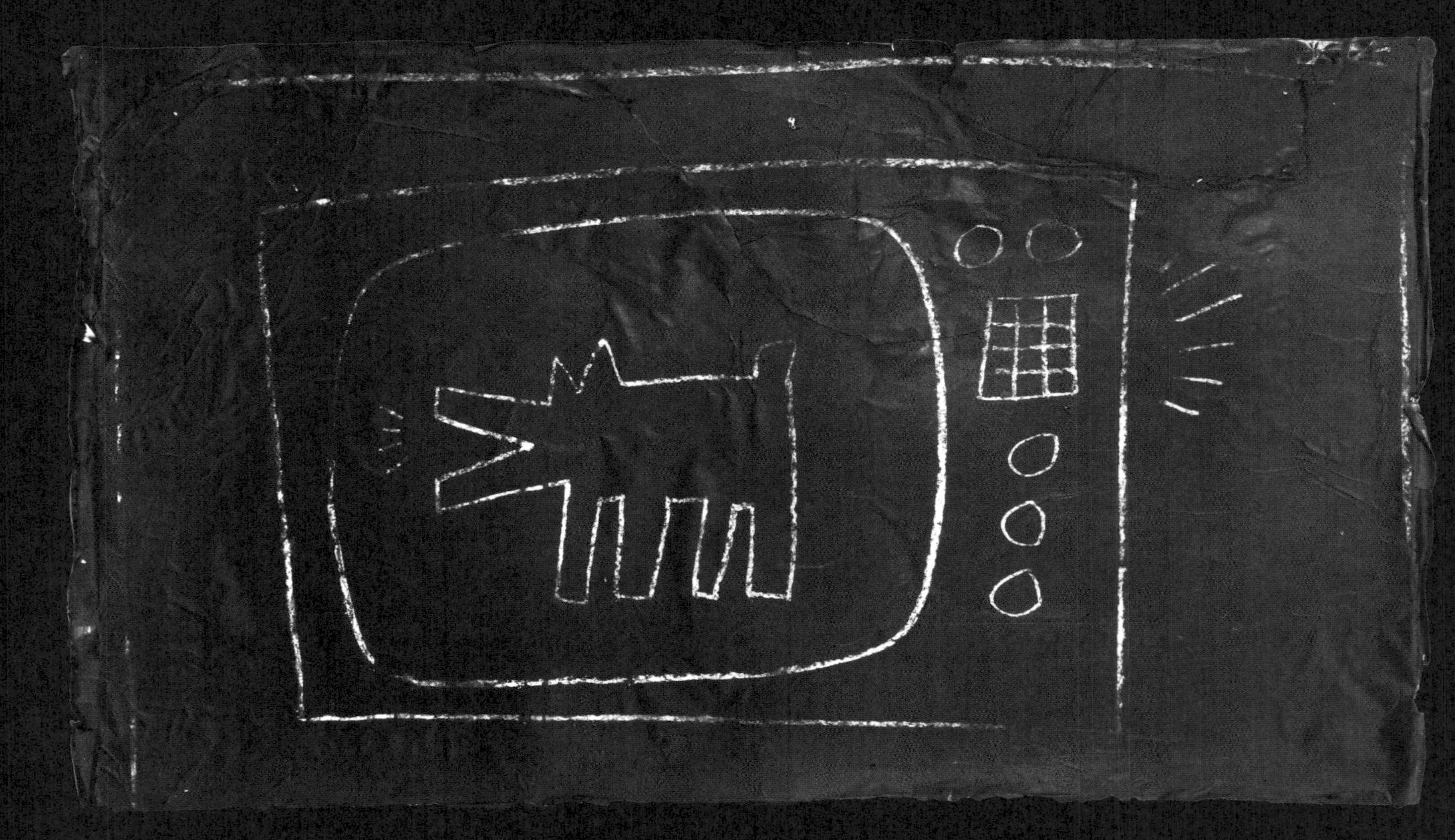

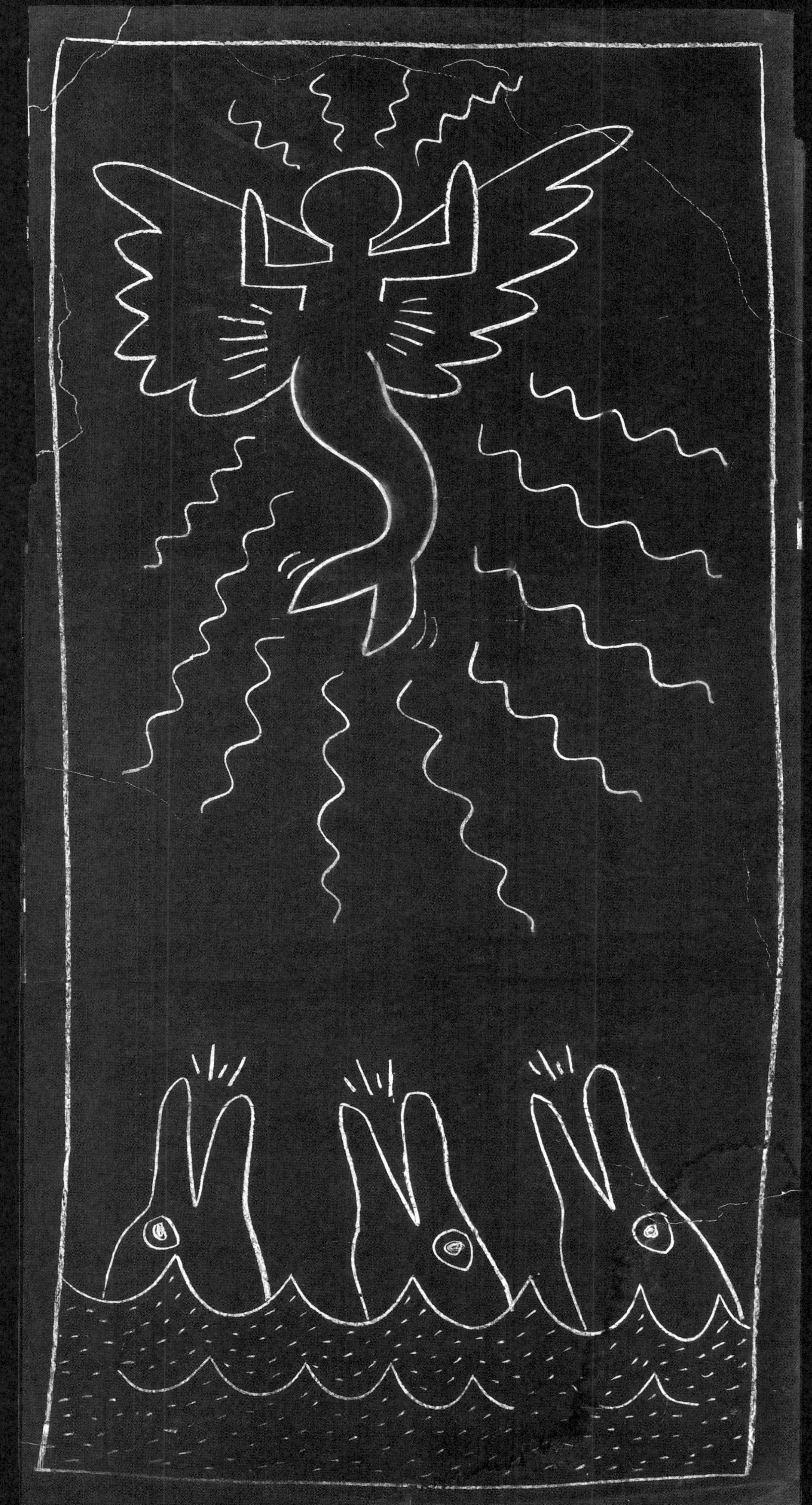

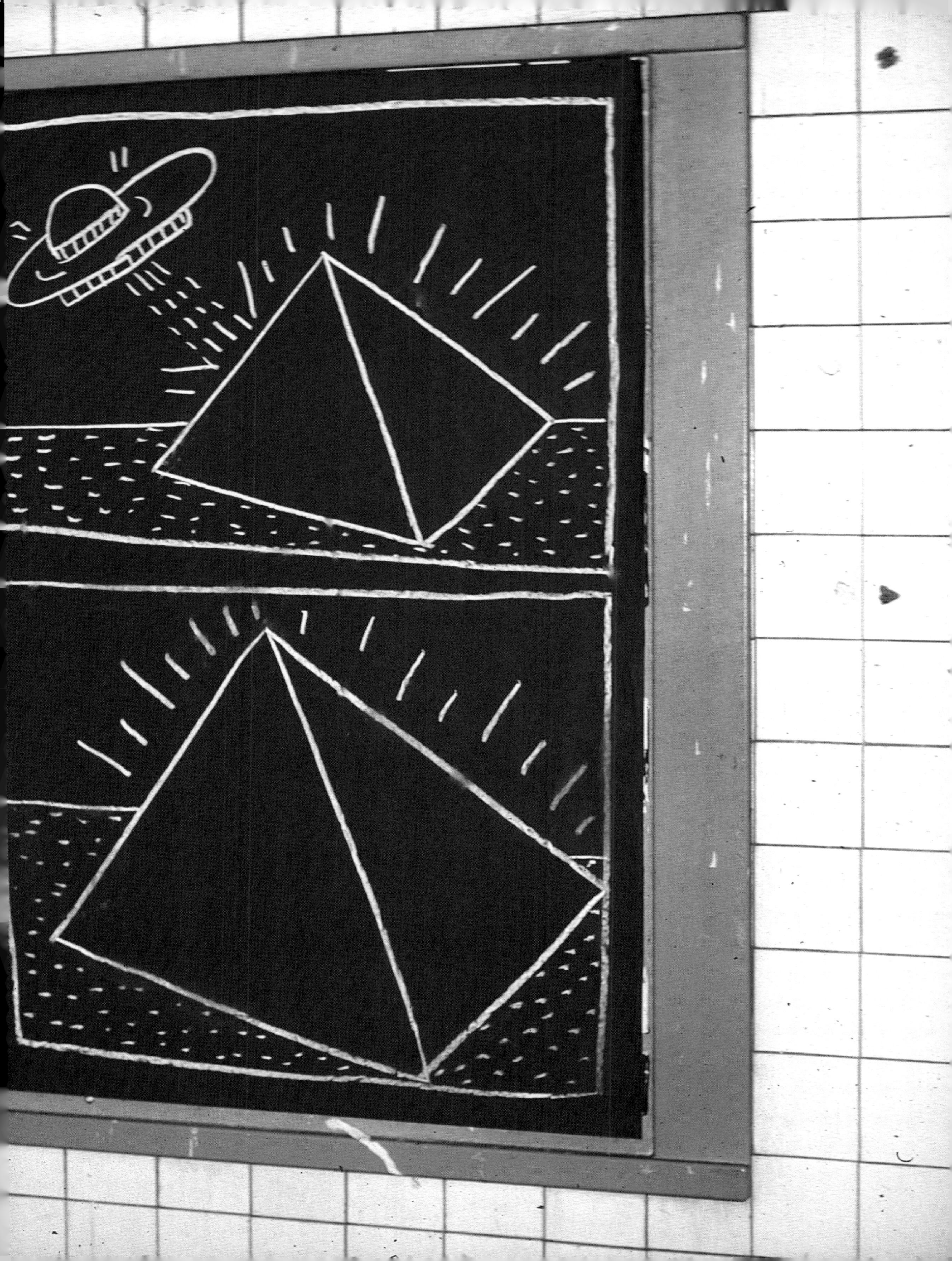

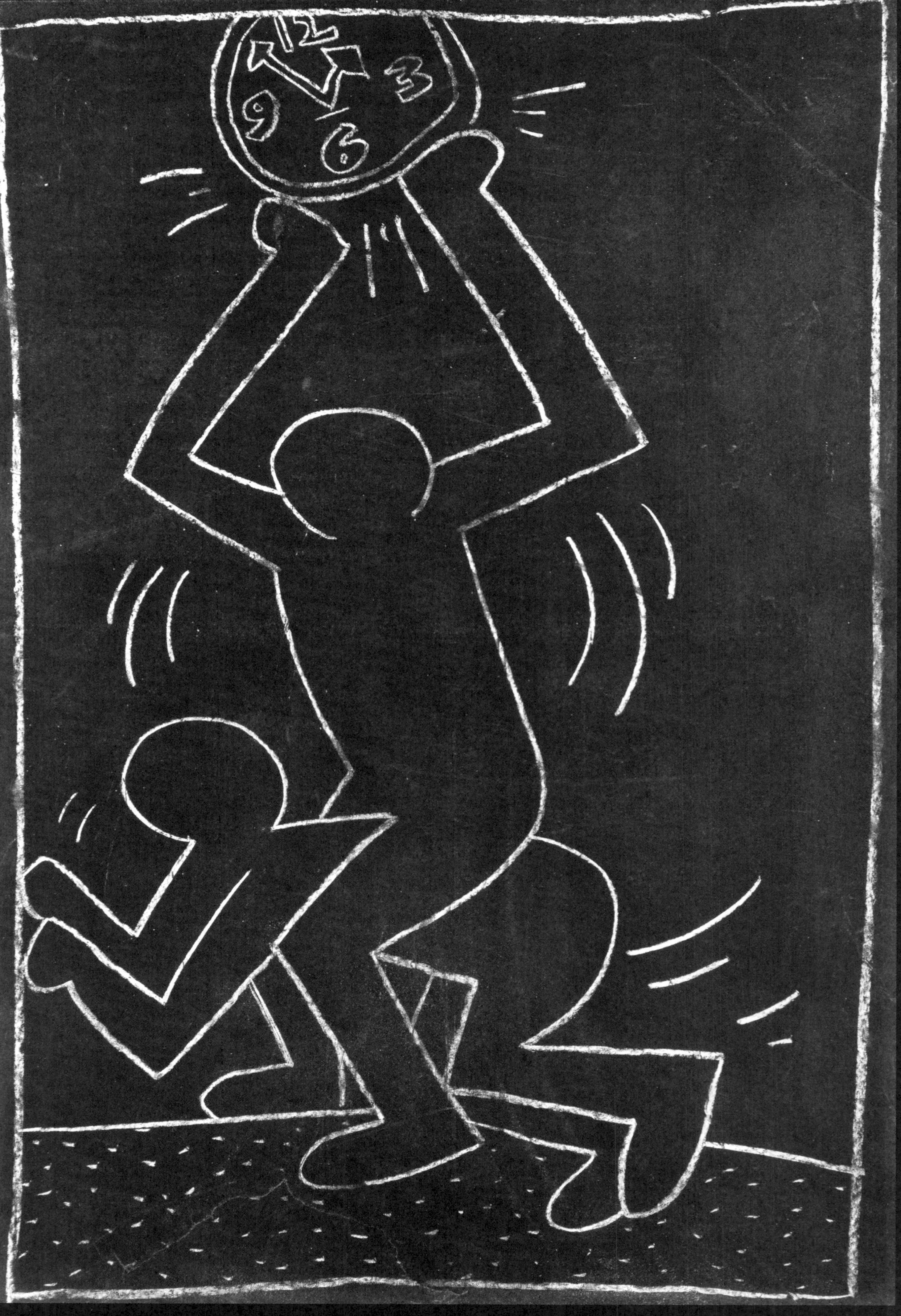

A Tuneful Celebration of Urban Commonality

Henry Geldzahler

The graffiti artists, or "writers" as they prefer to be called, graduate at any age between eleven and sixteen from the schools and sidewalks to that Olympic arena, public transportation. Enormous media attention has been focused on them. There has been, however, no unanimity of opinion on their value or on what their presence indicates about our society. What to one observer seems a healthy artistic outlet for rage, frustration, and the opportunity for identity in a culture which only "stars" are admired, is to another the unsightly defacement of public property — a Bronx cheer at government and authority.

Since the 1980s, a new presence has been seen and felt in New York City's street and subways. Radiant Babies, Barking Dogs, and Zapping Spacecraft, drawn simply and with great authority, have entered the minds and memories of thousands of New Yorkers. Our instant familiarity with this new pantheon of characters coincides with our rapid recognition that a sympathetic sensibility is at work in our midst. This call to attention, stronger than that exerted by the colossal glut of advertising or official signage, sets the work of Keith Haring apart from other graffiti writers. The man responsible for all this cheer never signs his work. Keith Haring's gift to the public is generous and heartfelt — a celebration of the spirit that is not and cannot be measured in dollars.

In the past two years, a parallel set of images has also been appearing in art galleries and museums. Fed by the same genius for the apt image and its inspired communication, Keith Haring's paintings in black and white and occasionally in Day-Glo green, oranges, and purples, have had immediate and international success when exhibited as fine art. It is this parallel career as a professional artist that has allowed Haring to continue his work in the streets and subways. Haring forces the fine art collectors of his work to subsidize the more public and unremunerated aspect of his activity. While this doesn't cause Haring the slightest confusion (he is perfectly able to harbor more than one idea at a time), the oversimplifiers wonder aloud: Does Keith Haring work for all New Yorkers or has he been coopted by the System, by exhibiting in commercial galleries and museums? The truth here, as so often, is not either/or; it is both at once.

Keith Haring's work appeals to us on several levels. First, of course, is the goofy cheerfulness that strikes immediately and, through repetition, becomes a leitmotif that sees us through our days — a tuneful celebration of urban commonality. When we spot the Radiant Baby or Barking Dog, we not only have seen them before and know we will see them again, we also know that tens of thousands of our fellows will see them as well.

Keith Haring has developed his own language, which speaks to us with immediacy in a deeply preverbal sense. Each term in this language can be read as subject, verb, or object: the Dog barks the Spacecraft or the Spacecraft zaps the Praying Man. In much the same way as Chinese or Egyptian languages are written pictographically, Keith Haring's world is made up of symbols that speak urgently to us, both alone and in interchangeable configurations. And as the pictographs or hieroglyphs communicate visually, soundlessly, so too are Haring's symbols swathed in silence. An eerie quietude surrounds all his work, heightening and animating the dramas they depict.

Behind an apparent ease of invention in Haring's work lies much visual knowledge and sophistication. As a child Keith Haring's ambition was to be a cartoonist and illustrator. His ease, fluency, and comic invention were astonishing at an early age. He enrolled in commercial art school in Pittsburgh but left after six months with a newfound dedication to the fine arts. It was in Pittsburgh, living on his own, that he happened on the Pierre Alechinsky exhibition at Carnegie Institute. Alechinsky in 1977 was a curious choice as the subject of a retrospective; his graphic style, which evolved in the 1950s, could not have seemed more out of phase in the minimalist preponderance of the late 1970s. In the elegantly agitated graphism of Alechinsky, Haring saw that expressionism (abstract and European at that) was again an option — an energetic prototype that could be absorbed and proffered again.

Haring hit upon the connections between his urgent cartoons and Alechinsky's equally agitated although less specific message. But he soon realized that to evolve from the abstract draftmanship that was engendered by this contact, a wider field of influence and stimulus was needed. It was specifically to enroll in the School of Visual Arts that Haring came to New York City in 1978. A quick study, he soon

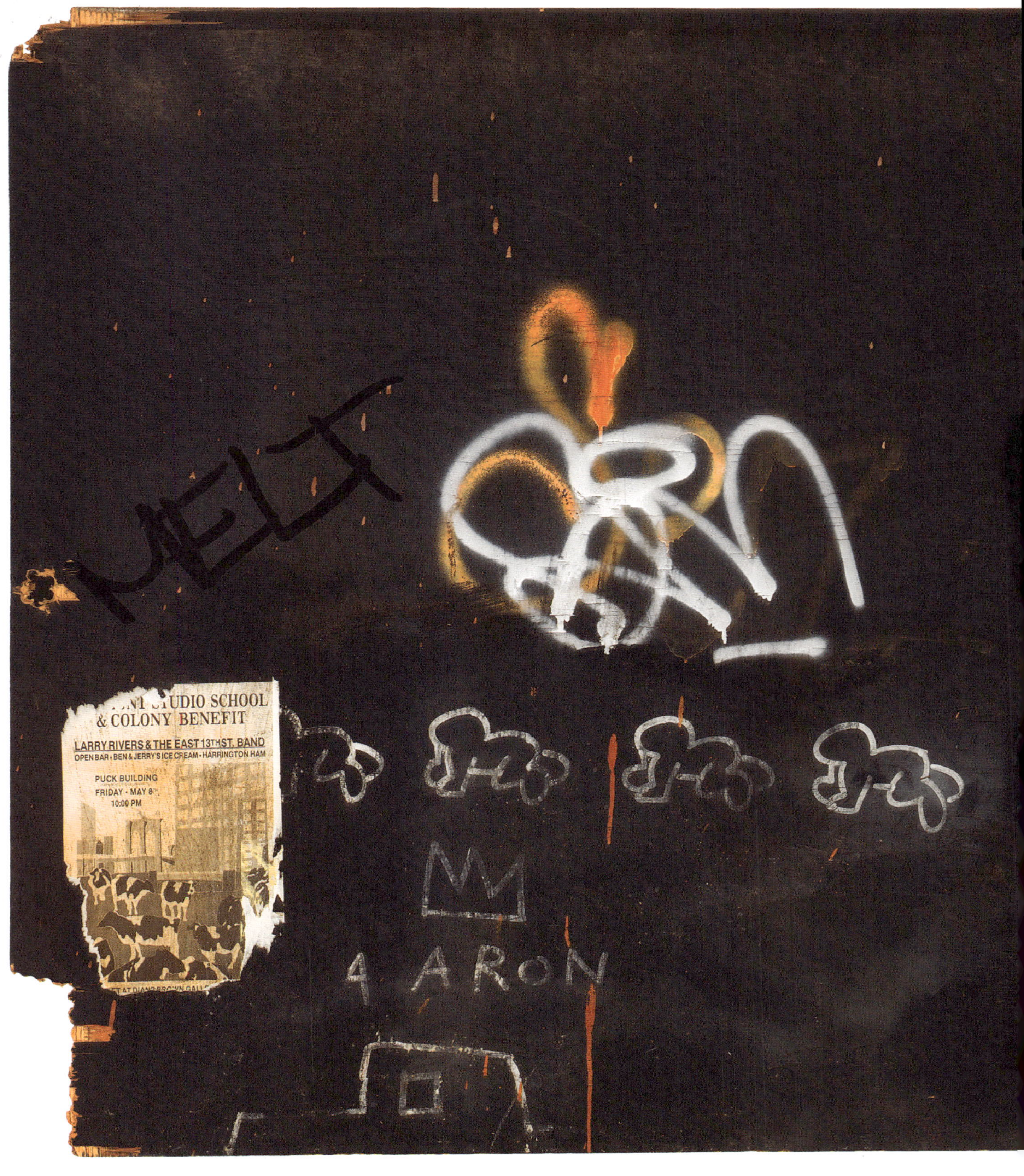

Keith Haring
collaboration with
Jean Michel Basquiat
Circa 1980 – 1983
Spray paint and
paper on plywood
48¼ x 86½ inches

absorbed and moved beyond the information, styles, and available attitudes at that curious institution, which is at once naive and hip. Ultimately, Haring's transition to the stunning new vocabulary of Pulsing Pyramids, Praying Figures and Hovering Angels was the result of a few months in New York City, driven by the hunger to communicate to a popular audience — one that lay outside the official art world.

What presuppositions lie behind Keith Haring's work? What exactly is his attitude toward his subject matter? Clearly, much sexual energy is abroad in his work — sexual energy being so powerful a part of our natures that in the healthy world Haring projects there is nothing to hide; indeed, exuberance abounds. Haring is acutely aware of this message in his work and keeps any specifically sexual images in the studio and out of the eye of the general public. "Kids like the drawings and I don't want to endanger that."

The terror and horror at the use of nuclear power and ever-present fear that through accident or intention an "incident" might occur are omnipresent in Keith Haring's drawings. (His hometown of Kutz-town, Pennsylvania, is only fifty miles from Three Mile Island.) The Spacecraft zaps a Pyramid, endowing it with radiant power; Running Men brandish pulsing bars of energy. Power is unleashed and manifests itself at all times and in every confrontation. Exchanges of energy from person to person and

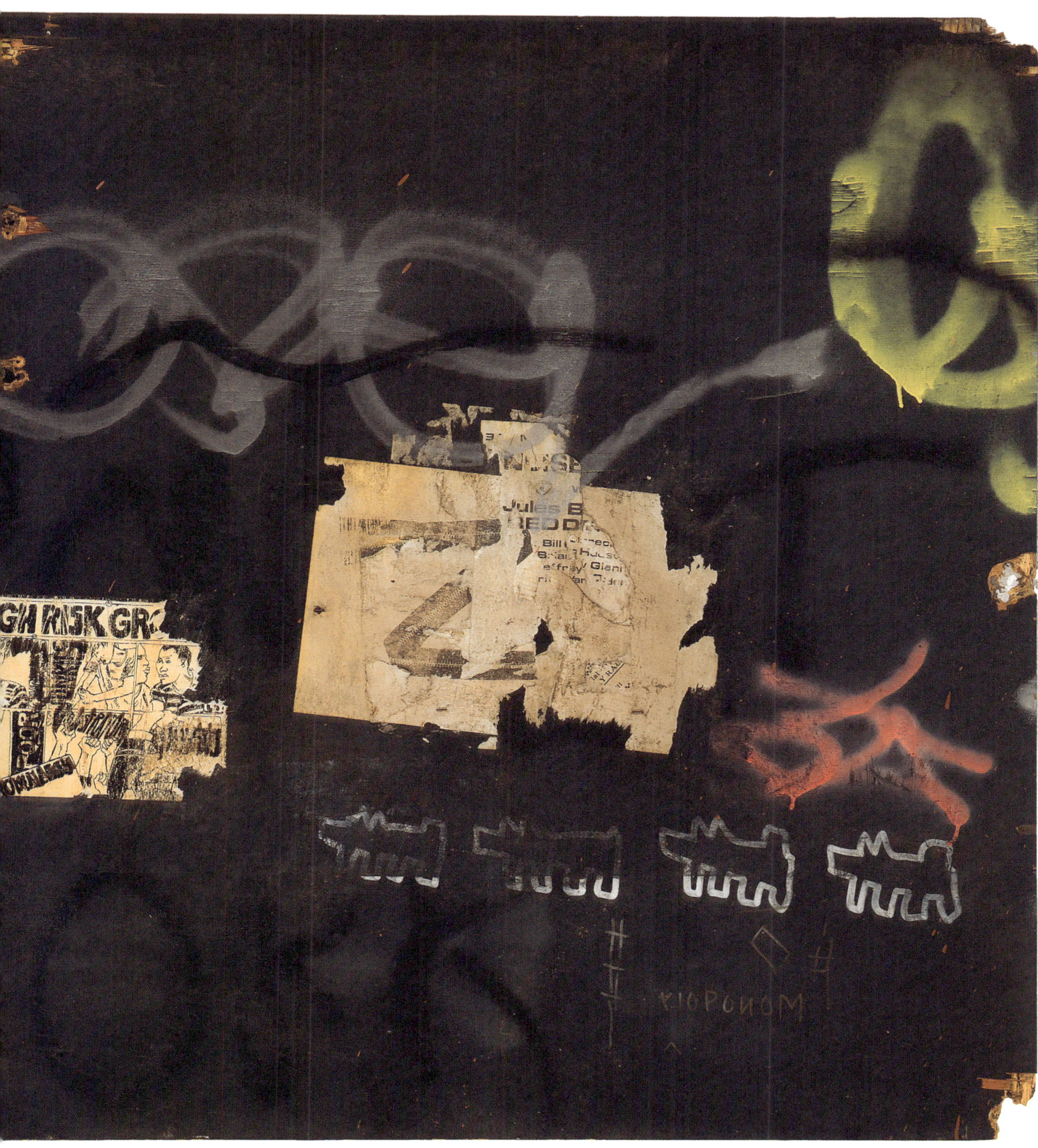

from "inanimate" objects to individuals are among the key transactions in all of Keith Haring's work.

Haring's sense of drama, of incident, is always strong and clear. Drawn in chalk on the black paper panels that the Metropolitan Transit Authority uses between rentals of advertising space, and in black sumi ink or Magic Marker on paper, oak tag, fiber glass, or vinyl tarpaulin, Haring's designs and prodigious inventiveness are always in the service of immediate, unmediated communication. The drama is so heightened that we often get the sense that the scene before us is a "still" from an action that has a past and a future. The toil involved in working up these scenes of great apparent spontaneity always takes place in the privacy of the studio.

Whether we are faced with a religious ceremony, a science fiction vignette, a love-dance, or a confrontation of antagonists, there is in all Keith Haring's work an intensified recognition of the drama of modern life; we can all identify with the Baby, the Dog and the Angel. In today's media-dominated world in which everyone is a Closet-Star, Keith Haring has managed brilliantly to picture a world with stark simplicity, sufficiently complex to allow every one of us a role. ∎

This essay was originally published in *Art in Transit: Subway Drawings* by Keith Haring; Photos by Tseng Kwong Chi; Introduction by Henry Geldzahler (Harmony Books, 1984). Reprinted with permission.

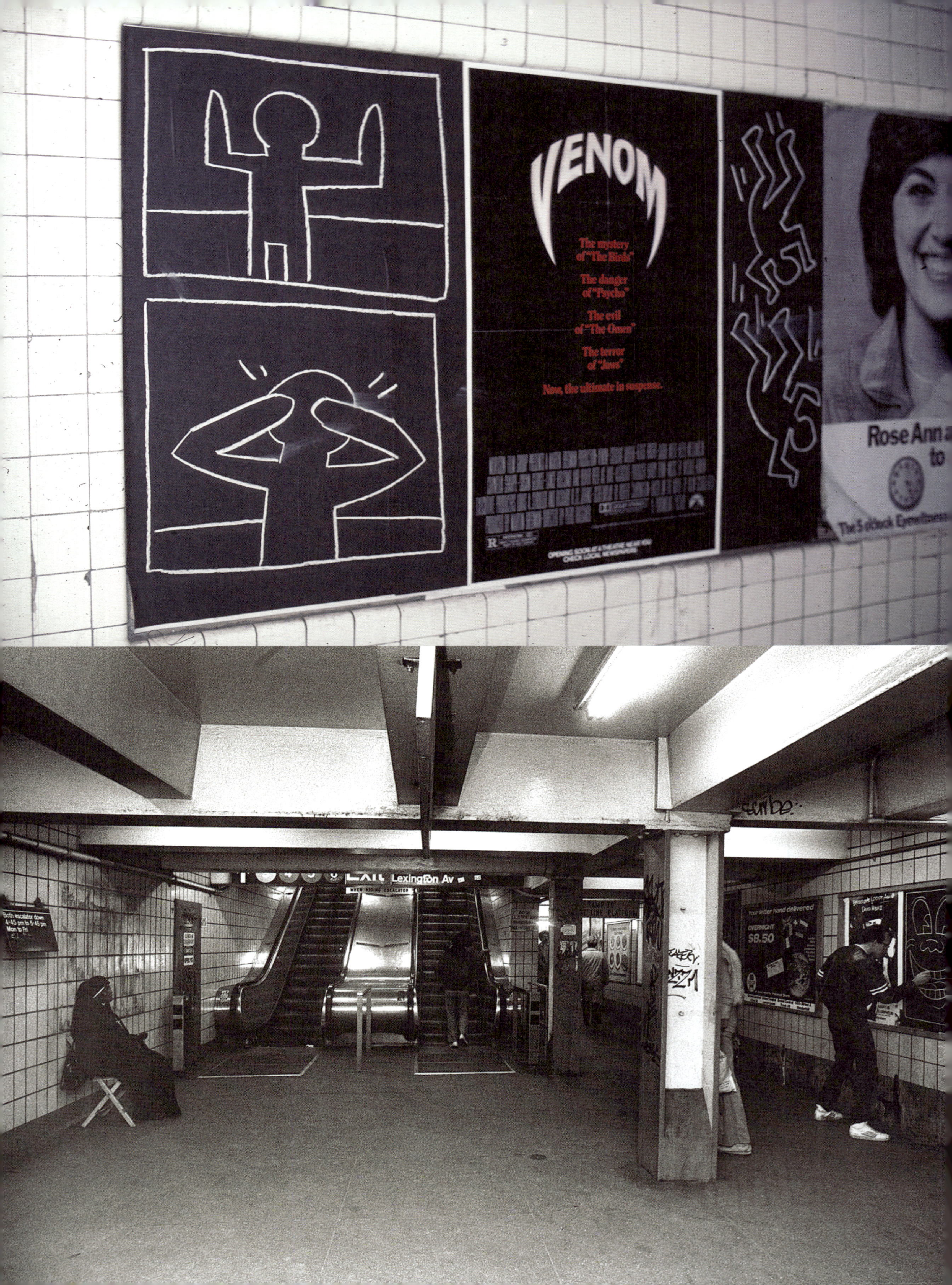
VENOM
The mystery of "The Birds"
The danger of "Psycho"
The evil of "The Omen"
The terror of "Jaws"
Now, the ultimate in suspense.
R
OPENING SOON AT A THEATRE NEAR YOU
CHECK LOCAL NEWSPAPERS
Rose Ann
to
The 5 o'clock Eyewitness
EXIT Lexington Av
WHEN RIDING ESCALATOR
Both escalator open
4:45 pm to 5:45 pm
Mon to Fri
Your letter hand delivered
OVERNIGHT
$8.50

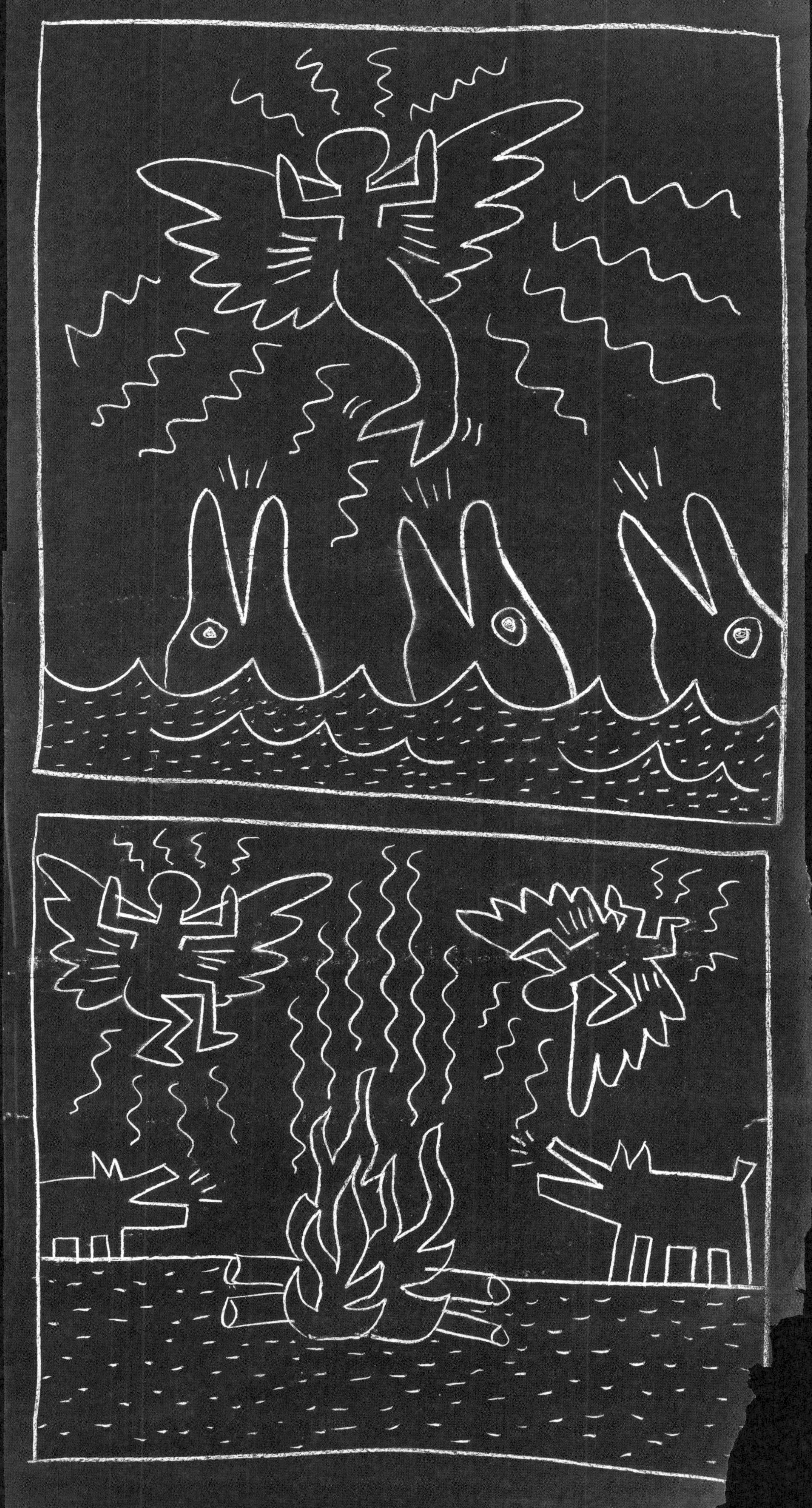

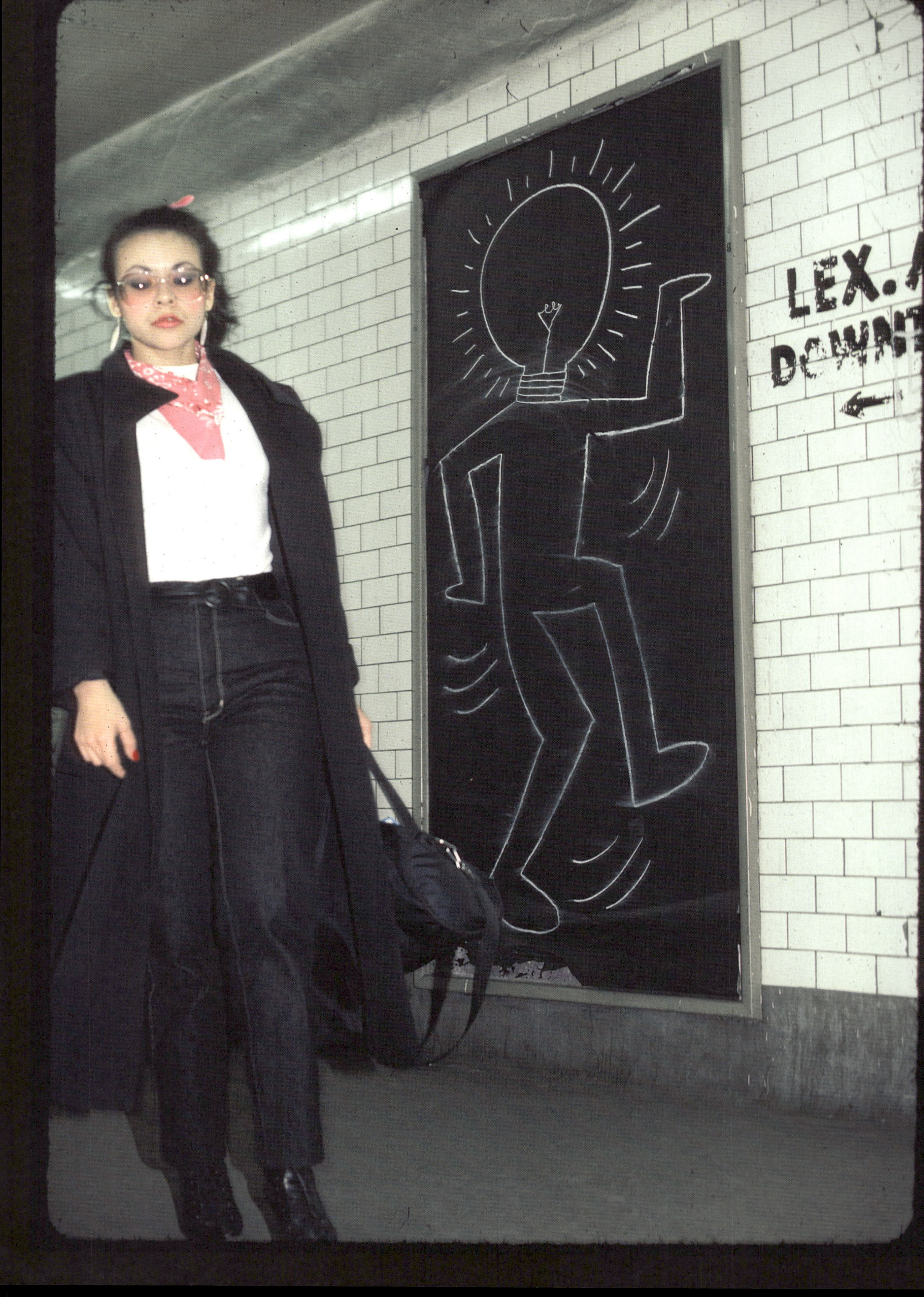

LEX.
DOWNT

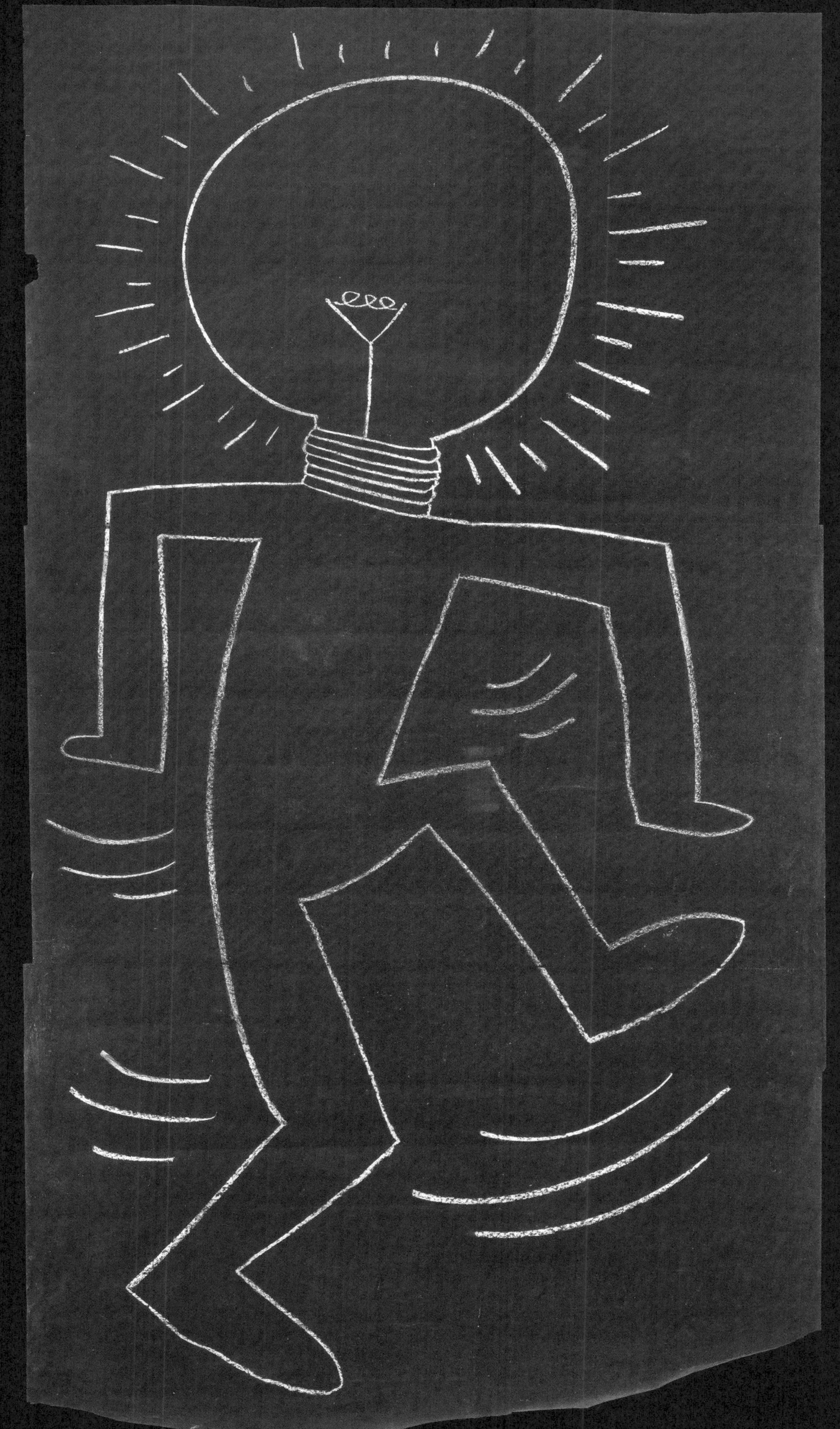

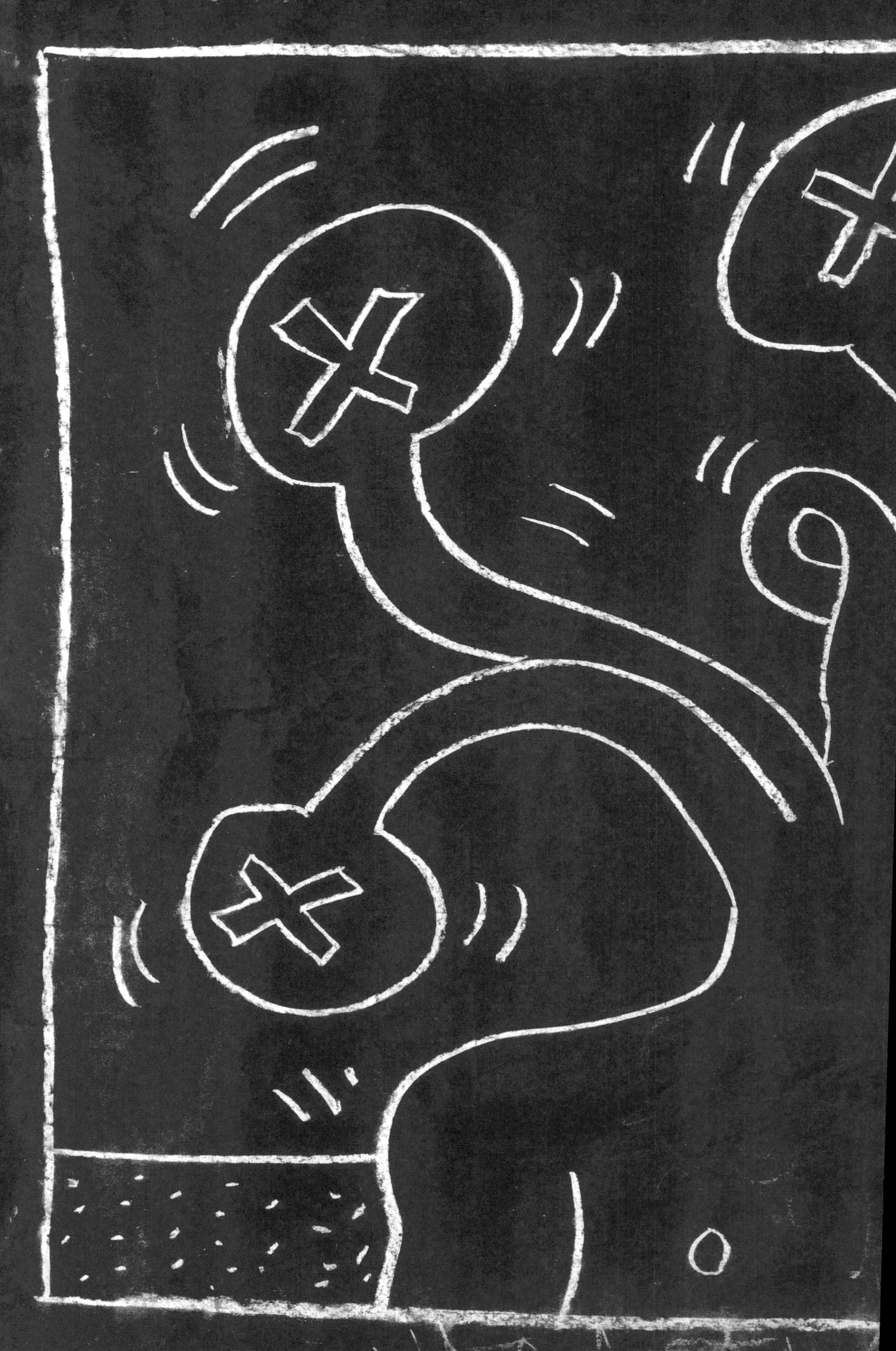

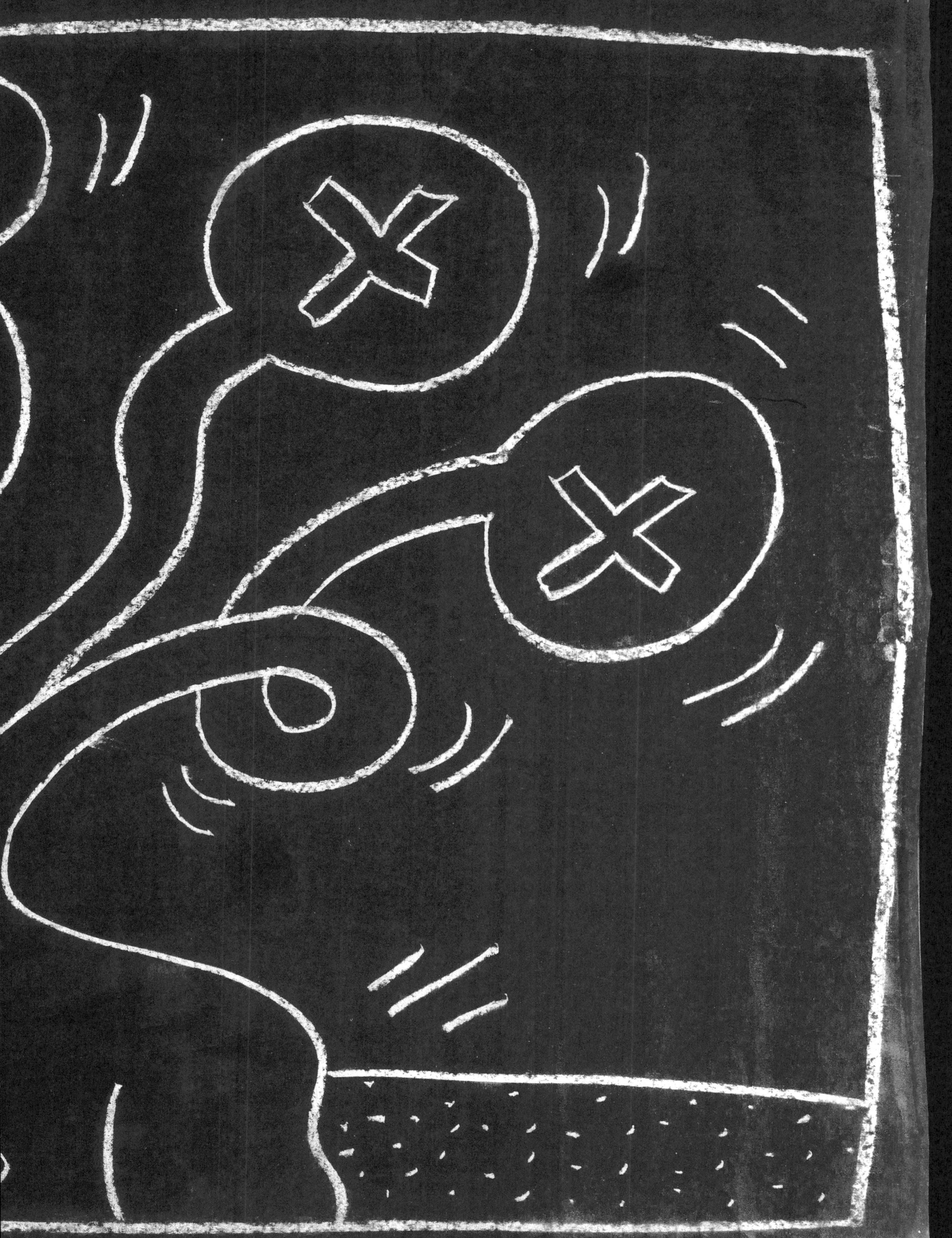

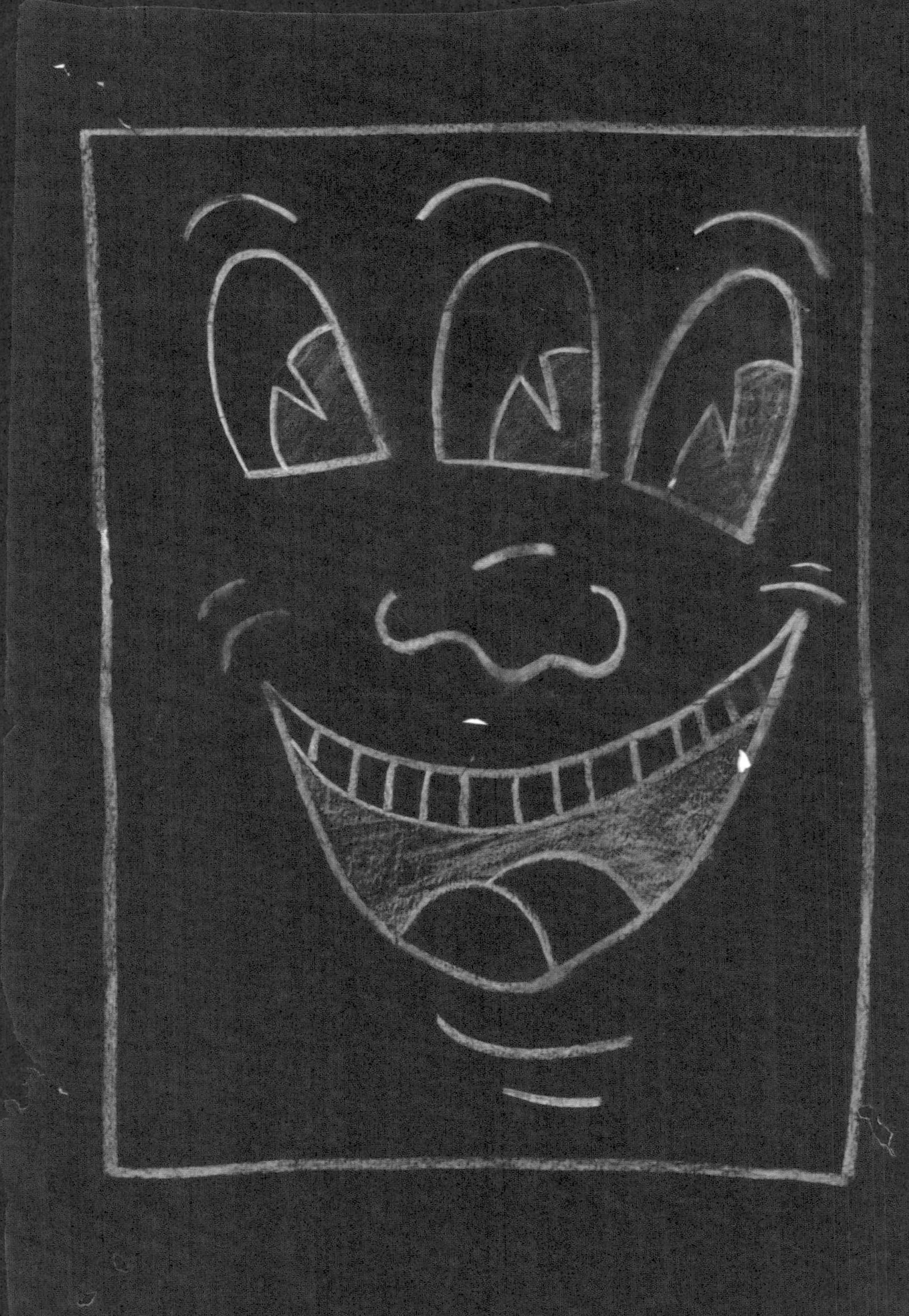

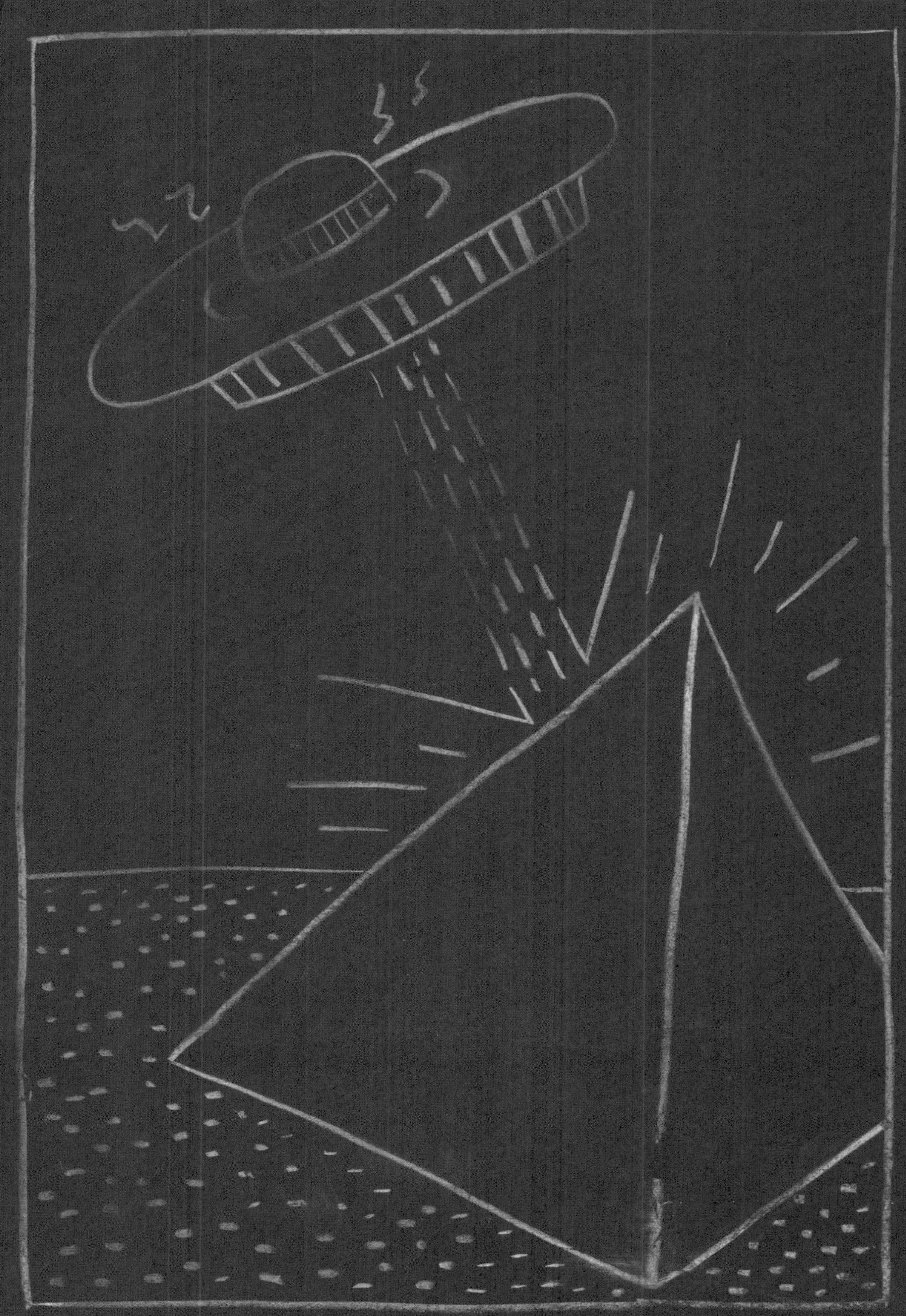

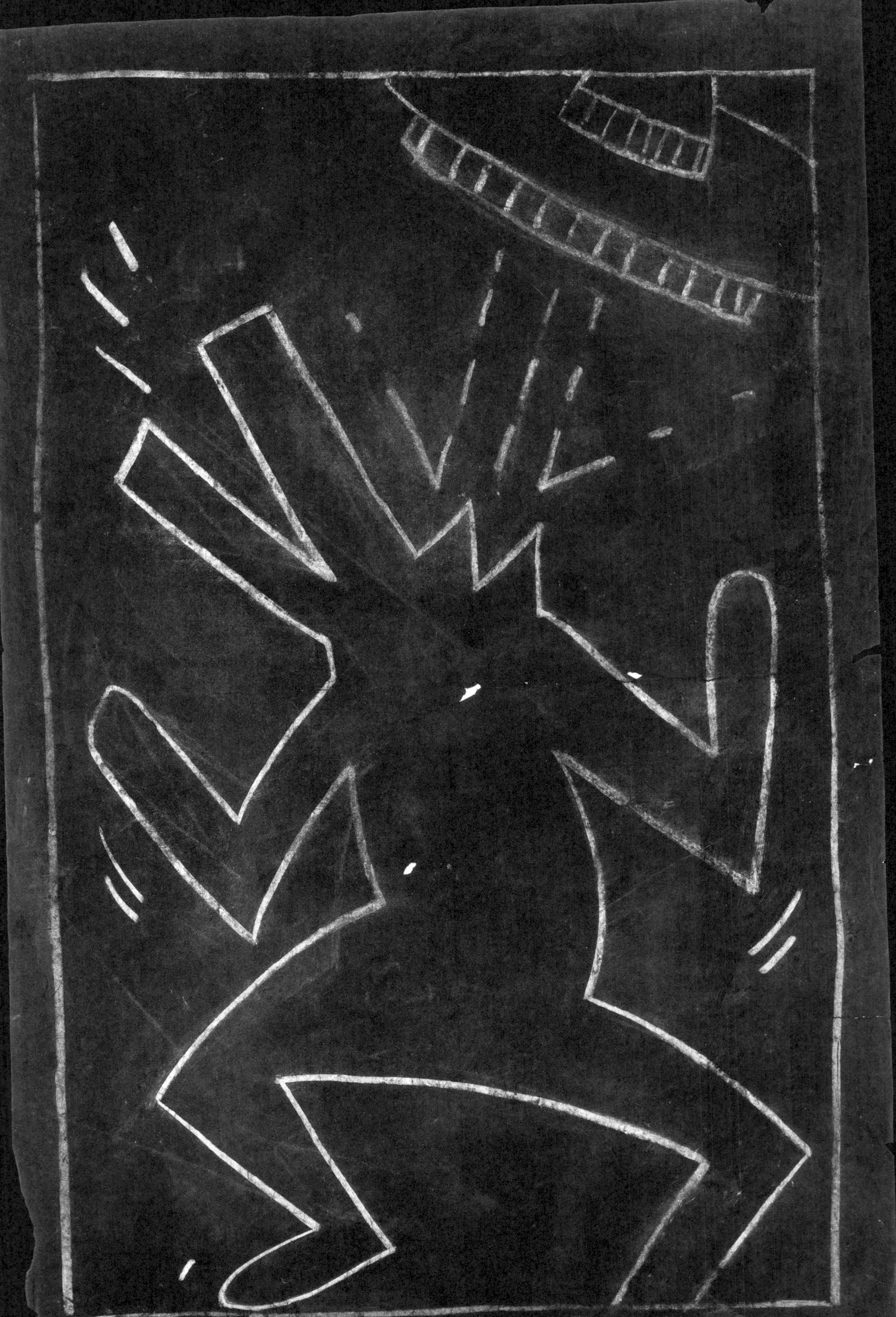

Why the Dogs Are Barking

Jeffrey Deitch

To thousands of tormented straphangers, it must appear that Satan is slowly penetrating the infrastructure of New York. It first became apparent that something was wrong about two years ago when dismembered *New York Post*-style headlines were suddenly pasted onto lamppost bases all over Manhattan. Blasting such prophetic screamers as "Reagan Slain By Hero Cop" and "Pope Killed For Freed Hostages" from hundreds of prime locations, they must have entered the consciousness of masses of stopped pedestrians. At least one civic-minded and obsessed observer was driven to the point of tearing around the city for hours, frantically scratching out the offending language.

Shortly thereafter, the mysterious chalk images began to appear below ground—scores of them. Deftly drawn on the black paper that the subway advertising company pastes over expired posters, they sprouted up in what seemed to be every station in town. Daisy chains of stubby babies and boxy dogs, at first seemingly cheery and upbeat, as fresh and frolicsome as Disney cartoons. The tumbling bodies, the gumby-like figures running up and down stairs vibrated with nervous energy. But juggled into one's visual inventory, the images slowly began to take on a subversive quality, projecting an aura of mental explosion and creeping doom. Masquerading as cartoons, they had thousands of subway riders a day studying sketches for Armageddon—drawings bubbling with unrestrained eroticism and spinning with signs of destruction.

And now these images are above ground too, the dogs and babies multiplying like rodents on doorways, dumpsters, and even on little buttons worn by skid row bums. A gigantic day-glo billboard packed with these madcap images barks out at motorists helplessly stopped for a red light at the corner of Houston and Bowery.

Do these strange images have some mysterious protector? The subway drawings couldn't be more vulnerable, just chalk on paper, but amazingly, they are hardly ever tampered with. The delicate images remain untouched while nearly every Frank Perdue ad is a constant target for all sorts of desecration. The white on black drawings seem to have an immunity like that of a frail priest walking through the toughest slum. An unknown power keeps opposing forces at bay.

New Yorkers who take notice of the city's visual eccentricities must wonder what in the world is going on down there. What sort of cult could be systematically hitting subway stations everywhere with new images almost weekly, scattering radiant babies everywhere. Those with a Manichean tendency must see the Devil's work: Satan slowly expanding his grip on the consciousness of the vulnerable. There must even be people who actually worship these images, descending into the subways at night to perform obscure religious rituals. A new obsession has been implanted into the life of a city swirling with men and women obsessed. Keith Haring—artist— has created a phenomenon that has not only covered thousands of surfaces, but has entered thousands of minds. Like the crazed woman who etches "Pray" on every pay telephone in town, like the chicken- headed Frank Perdue on posters everywhere, like Luciano Pavarotti on the stage of the Metropolitan Opera, Haring has become part of the culture of New York City.

Yet in an environment where mass attention is nothing special, it's amazing that Haring is one of the few artists to take advantage of the opportunity to cut out the middlemen and deal direct. Going public for Haring does not involve compromise or a watering down of his art's integrity. With him it's just the opposite; his public approach in fact eliminates many of the barriers that constrain other artists. Haring has never had to wait around for someone to offer him a show. The art goes right up whenever it's ready, and it just pours out. Squirming with nervous energy, Haring puts out the art wherever he is: on the streets, the subways, on schoolyard walls. Getting gallery shows has never been a problem, either. Haring just organizes his own: at Club 57, the Mudd Club, or whatever other space happens to be conveniently accessible.

Haring's unbridled determination to get the art out is contagiously exciting, but that's only where the aesthetic interest begins. He has a sense for location and context, for instance, that's as good as that of any space buyer at J. Walter Thompson. The lamppost bases were easily the most effective locations in the city for Haring's deranging *Post* headline knock-offs. The pieces remained up for months without ever being covered over, continuous targets for the wandering eyes of every pedestrian. Positioned as they were with no visual competition from other signs or placards, they were starkly effective. Going below ground, Haring's subway "blackboards" are

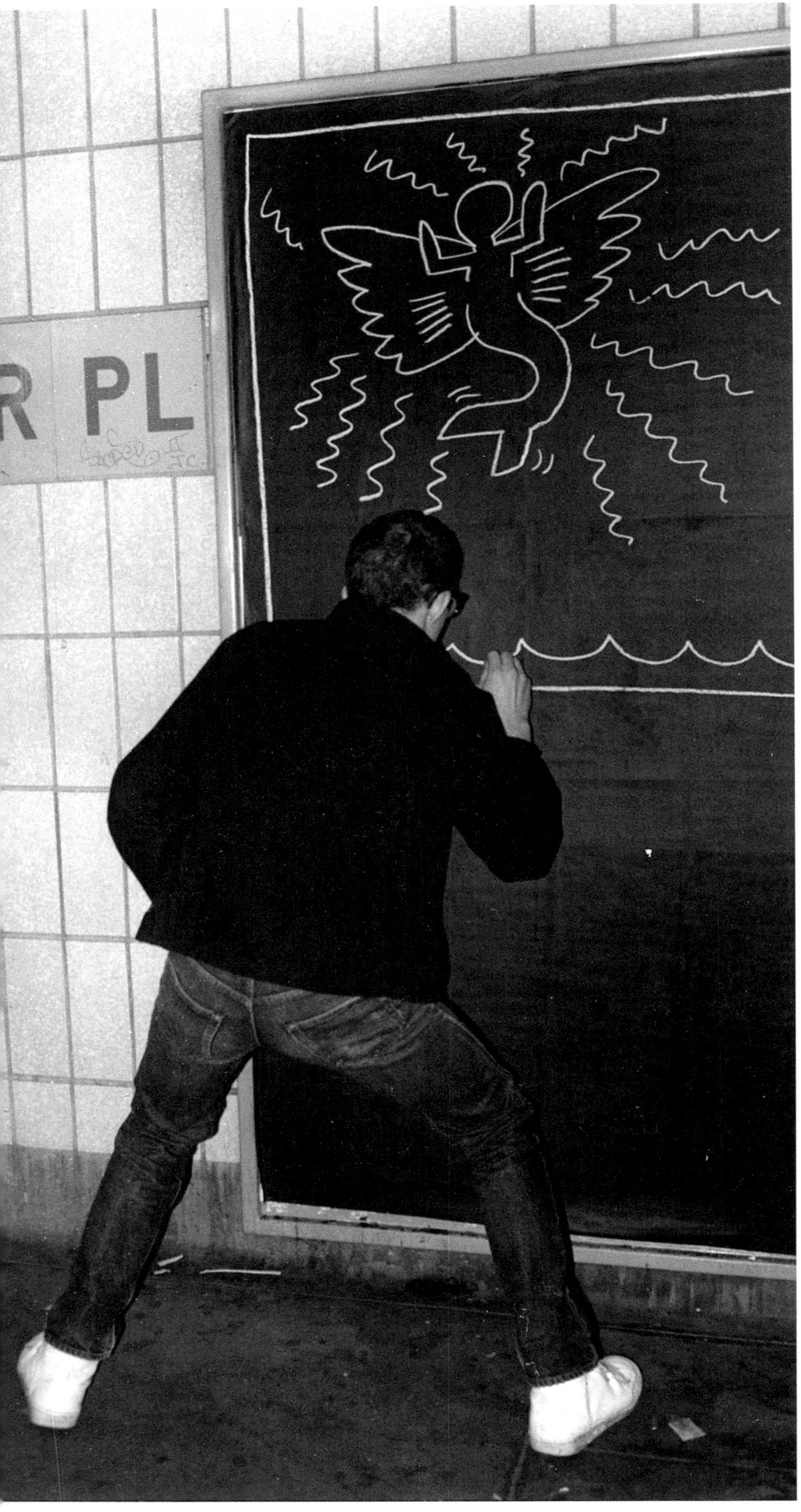

his contextual triumph. How odd that the subway advertising company so neatly and precisely covers up expired ads with those clean black sheets. And how odd that for years, until Haring came along, the black spaces just remained there without really being noticed. In exploiting such obscure spots that are so obvious after the fact, Haring is as effective as Daniel Buren, the art context specialist. Haring's recent billboard at the corner of Houston and Bowery isn't on just any wall. It is painted onto a peculiar slablike rectangle that just stands there, stuck into a tiny abandoned triangle of land. The wall's bizarre useless quality, inches away from the neighboring building, but not attached, gives the piece an especially activated quality. Actually, Haring's most innovative use of space was neither on the streets nor the subways, but on his eyeglass frames. Until they became hopelessly encrusted with paint, Haring would give his artist friends solo exhibitions on his spectacles at the rate of around one a week. Every time you ran into Haring it was an art experience.

It's not just Haring's locations, but his media, which are so cleverly chosen: drawing with chalk in the subway, for instance. The most vulnerable medium in existence is thrust into the most vulnerable location in New York. Even armed cops don't always feel safe in the subways. Haring's firm but delicate drawings have a special impact, surviving as they do in their brutal environment. They wouldn't be nearly as effective in a more permanent medium like spray paint.

Although Haring has a brilliant grasp of the power of the context and media, it's of course the images themselves that make the work so extraordinary. On the surface they are childishly simple, almost notations rather than real drawings. They are by necessity conceived for speed of execution as well as for audience readability. Haring whips out a panel in two minutes flat before he runs down the platform to throw up another. The drawings are

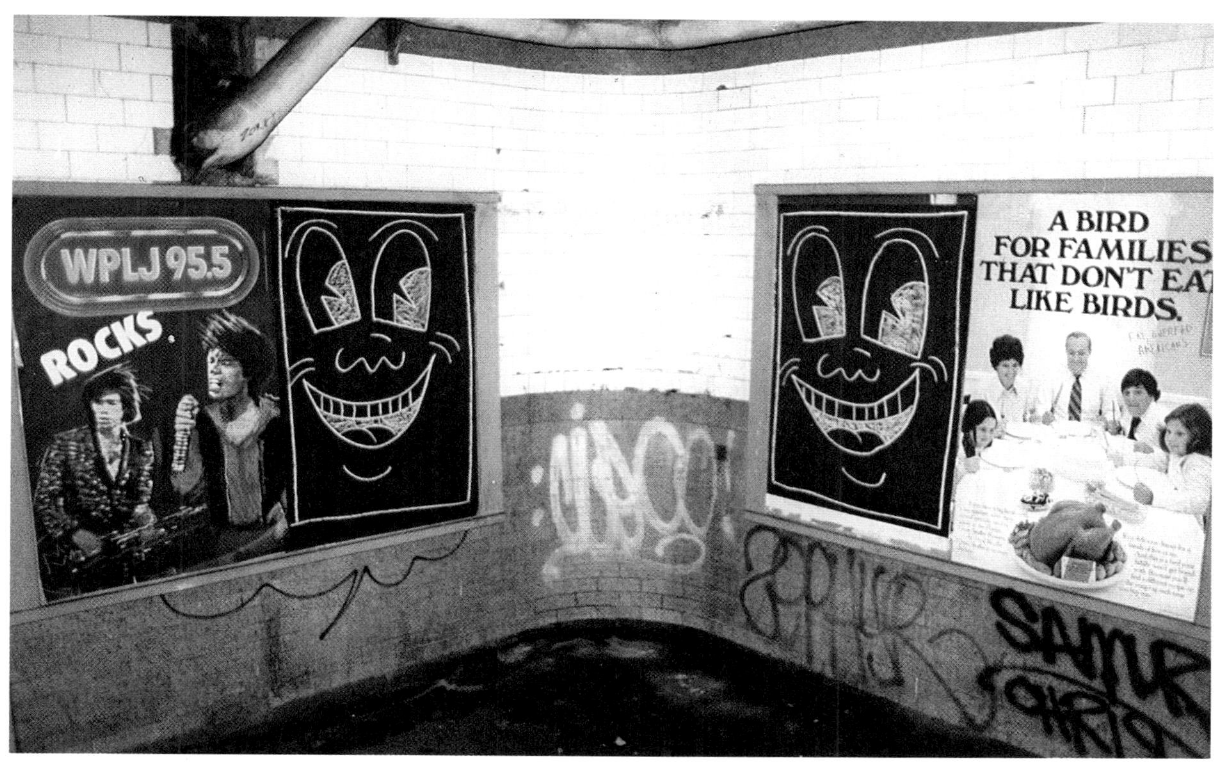

designed as well for split-second comprehension. A commuter will rush by three or four while running toward the turnstiles, taking them in at a speed reader's pace. Dozing subway riders catch glimpses of the panels through the car windows as the express barrels through a local station. And that is not to say that the images aren't studied carefully day after day by some of the more aesthetically oriented members of the subway community.

Haring is one of the few artists since the Pop Art era who has been able to successfully integrate America's great commercial art form — cartooning — into fine art. That does not mean just putting up haywire images of Mickey Mouse, but means adopting the techniques of celluloid animators to communicate with startling effectiveness. By repeating his images over and over again in multiple frames, Haring has in effect created a giant walk-through cartoon show all over the city. Of course, even without Keith Haring the city would still be a giant cartoon show, but that itself makes the work even more appropriate.

One can be tempted to analyze Haring's images from a semiotic point of view. The stubby crawling baby, for instance, reads not just "baby," but such things as human vulnerability, a sense of unfettered freedom associated with a baby's developing consciousness, and a polymorphous sexuality. One could make a similar analysis of Haring's entire images vocabulary. His images are insightfully chosen and carefully worked out with a sensitivity toward layers of meaning and sexual connotation. They are not just drawings, but "signs." But these rings of meaning around the individual figures are only part of the Haring process.

The work's full impact results from a melange of all these elements — context, medium, imagery — and their infiltration into the urban consciousness. Individual frames may appear perfectly innocent, but taken together, Haring's works have a quality of menace, a sense of impending violence, and of sexual explosion. They diagram the collective unconscious of a city—a city that moves along happily enough, but just barely enough to keep from degeneration into the dog-eat-dog, topsy-turvy world of Haring's images. Haring's image of an outsized atom bouncing across the screen of a TV set illustrates our strange situation particularly well.

Life is still full of fun on the surface, but underneath it all, the specter of nuclear destruction creeps closer and closer. We can still frolic around like Haring's little babies, but the barking of the dogs becomes louder and louder.

There are cynics who view Haring's public works merely as clever, free advertisement for his "real" art that is told in the galleries. And of course one can take the opposite view and interpret his gallery pieces merely as funding source for his "real" work, his work on the streets. Haring's actual approach is certainly quite a bit more complex. Like Andy Warhol and Christo, he is unconstrained by the boundaries of the traditional artist's role and is seeking to develop a role of his own. Meshing Madison Avenue and Walt Disney with systematic and contextual art, and laying it all onto a graffiti beat, Haring is creating more than good paintings and drawings. He's not just making art; he's communicating in a totally contemporary way. ■

Adapted from an essay that originally appeared in the exhibition catalogue Keith Haring *(Tony Shafrazi Gallery, October 1982). Reprinted with permission.*

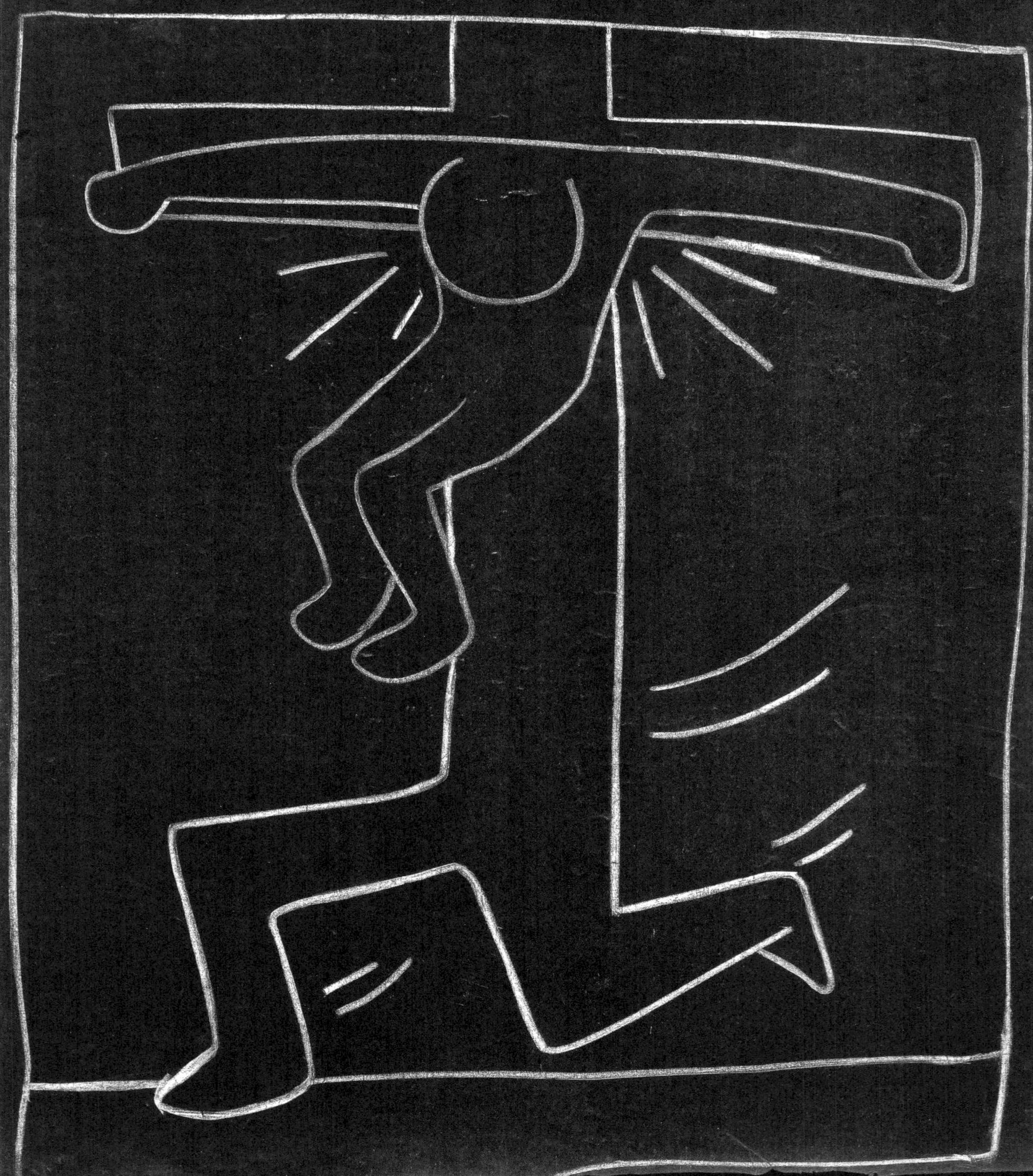

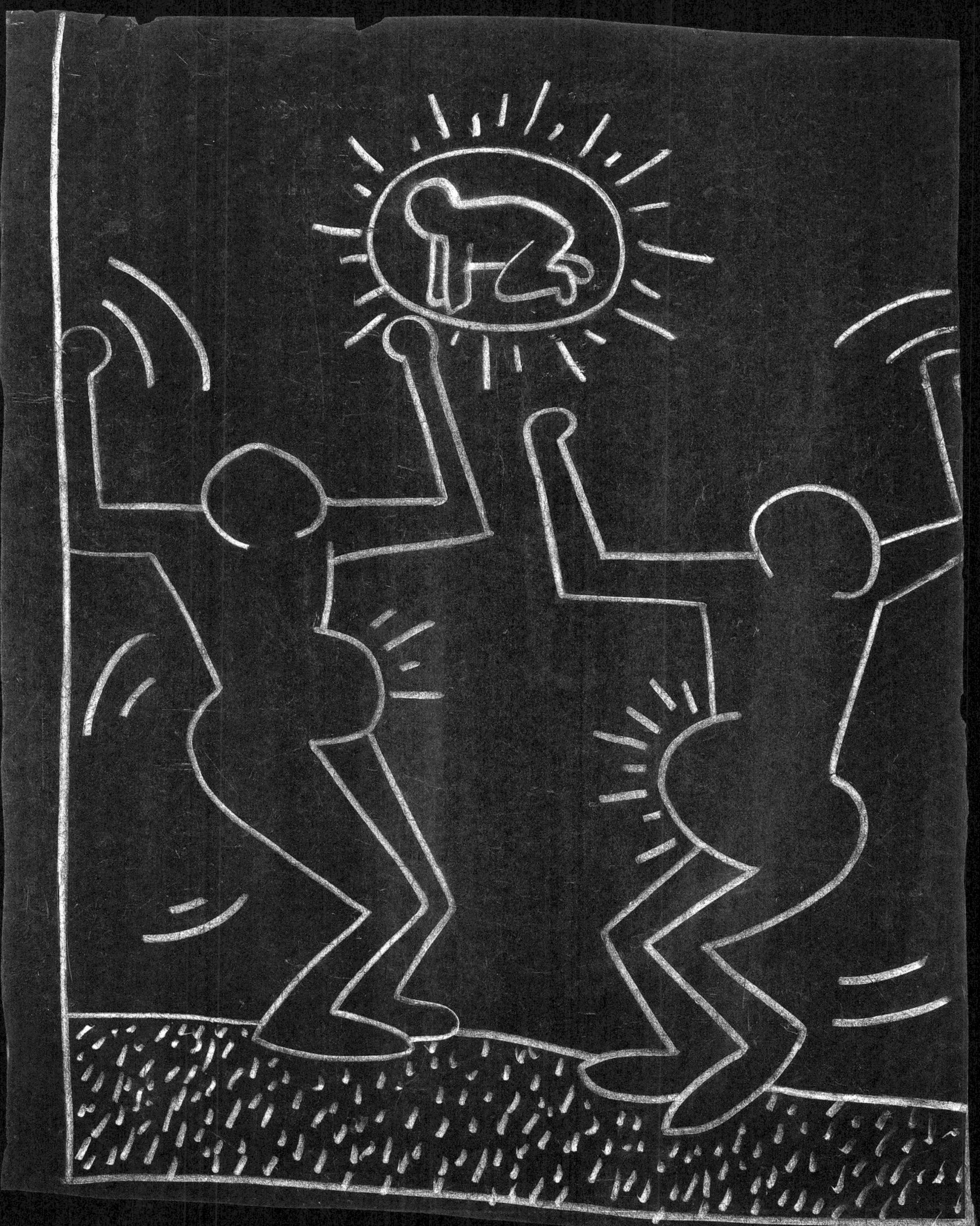

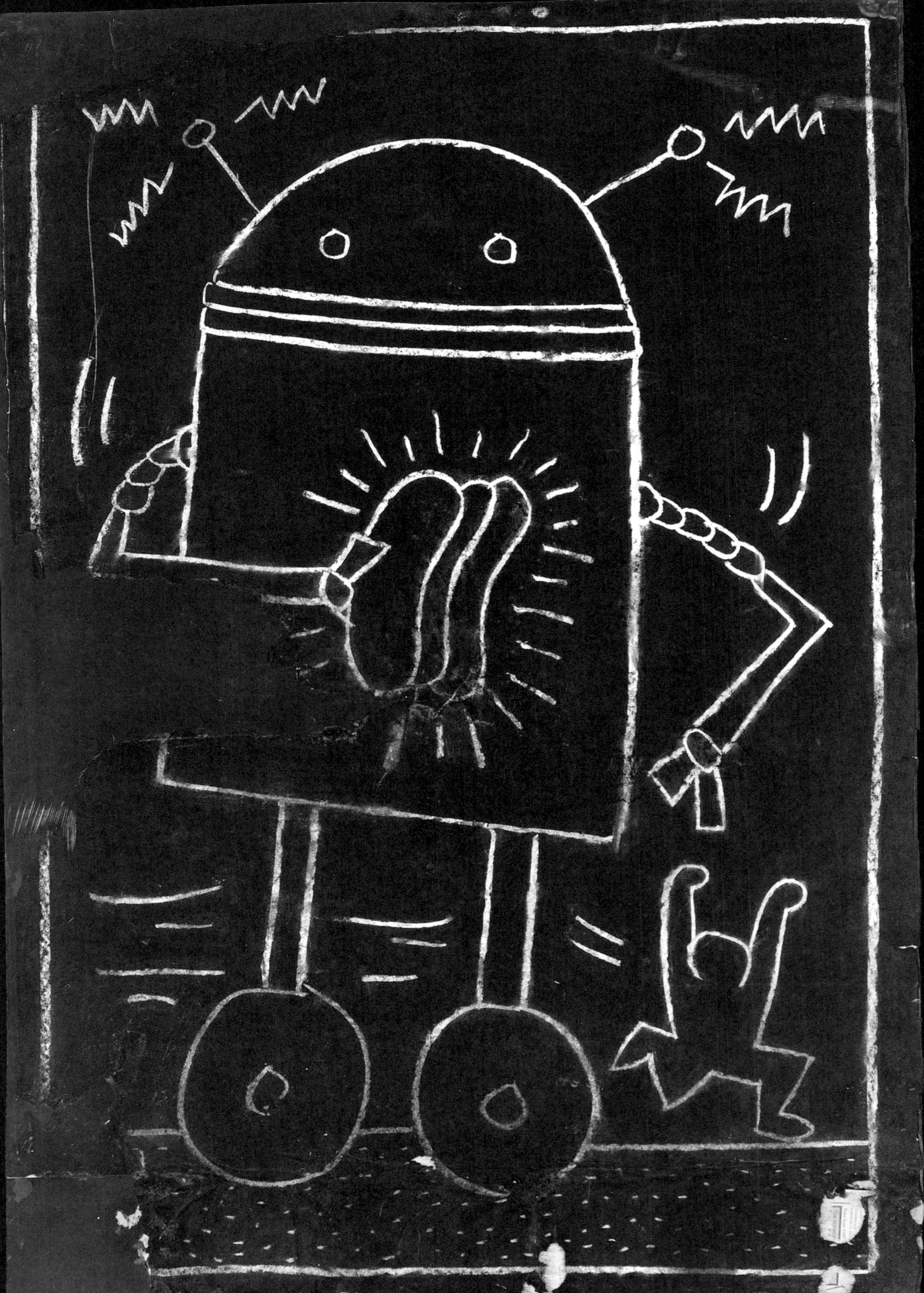

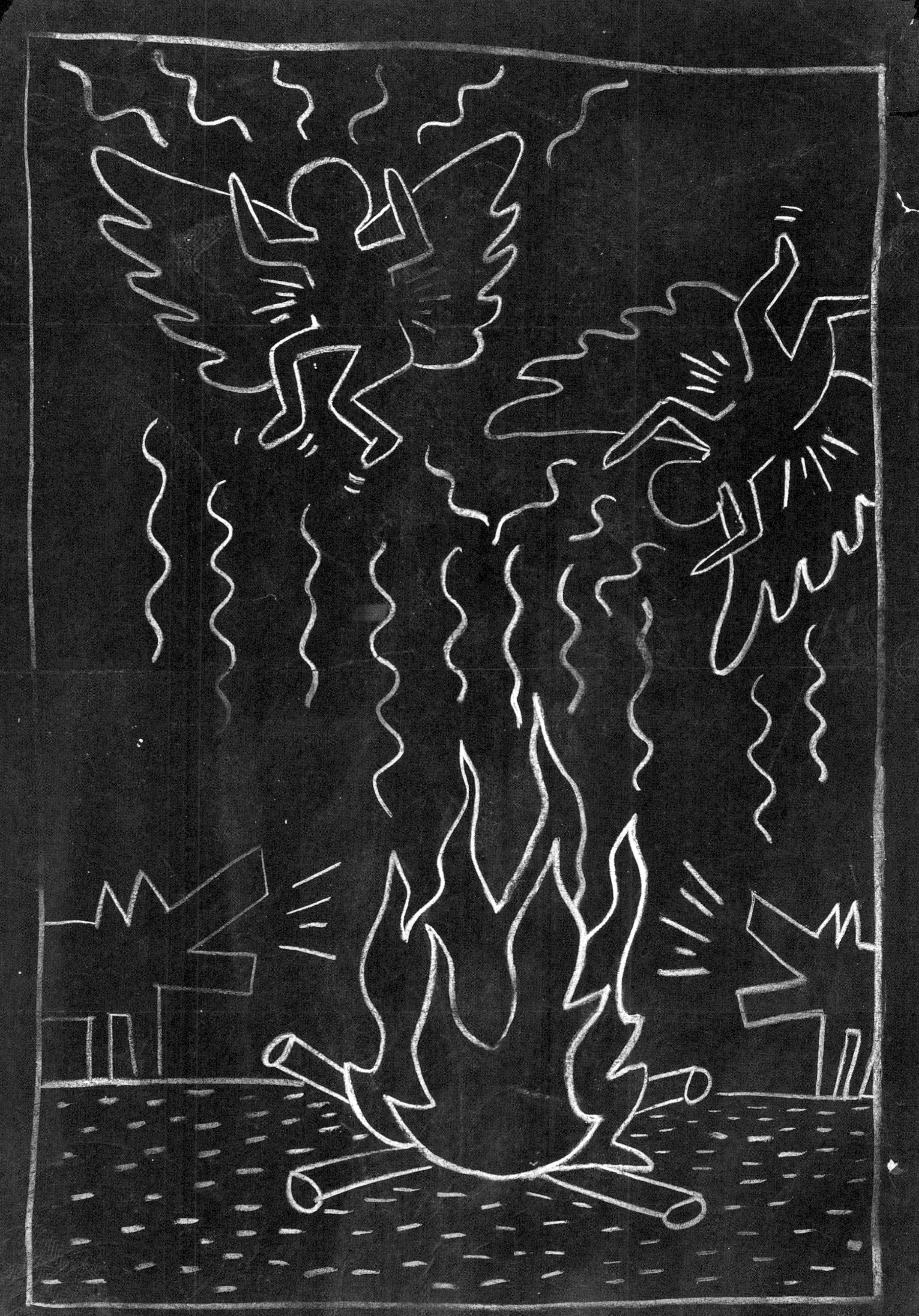

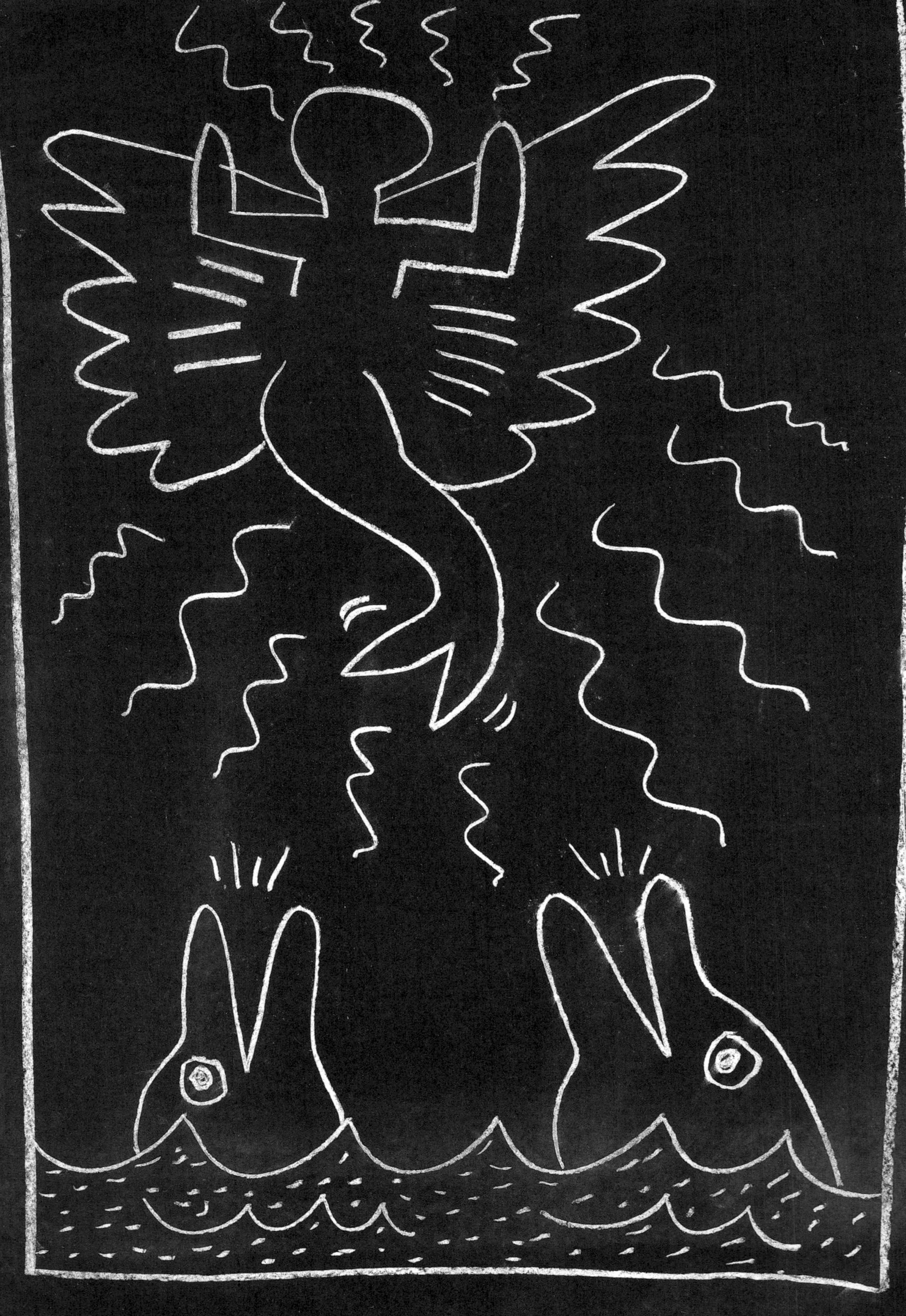

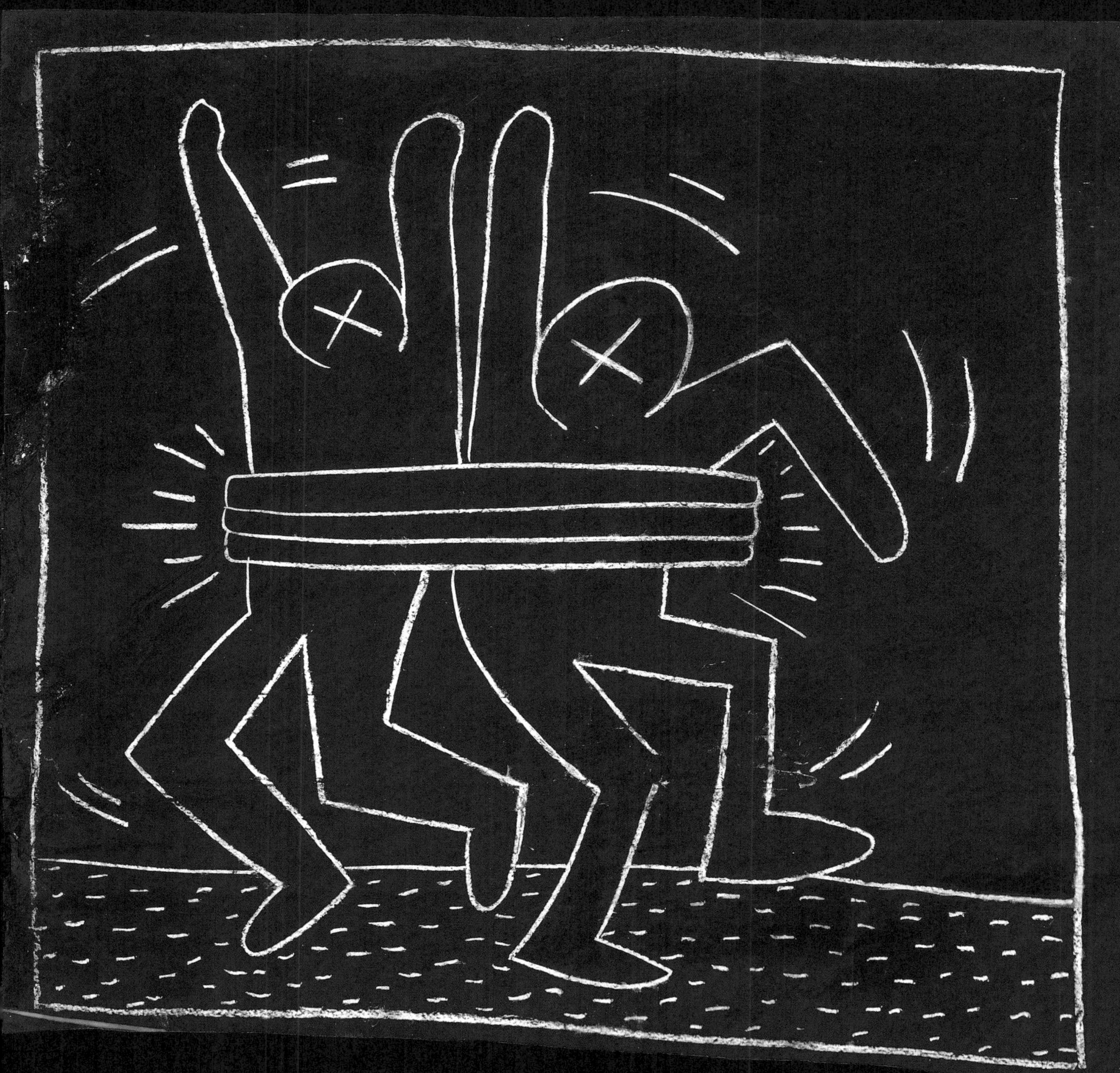

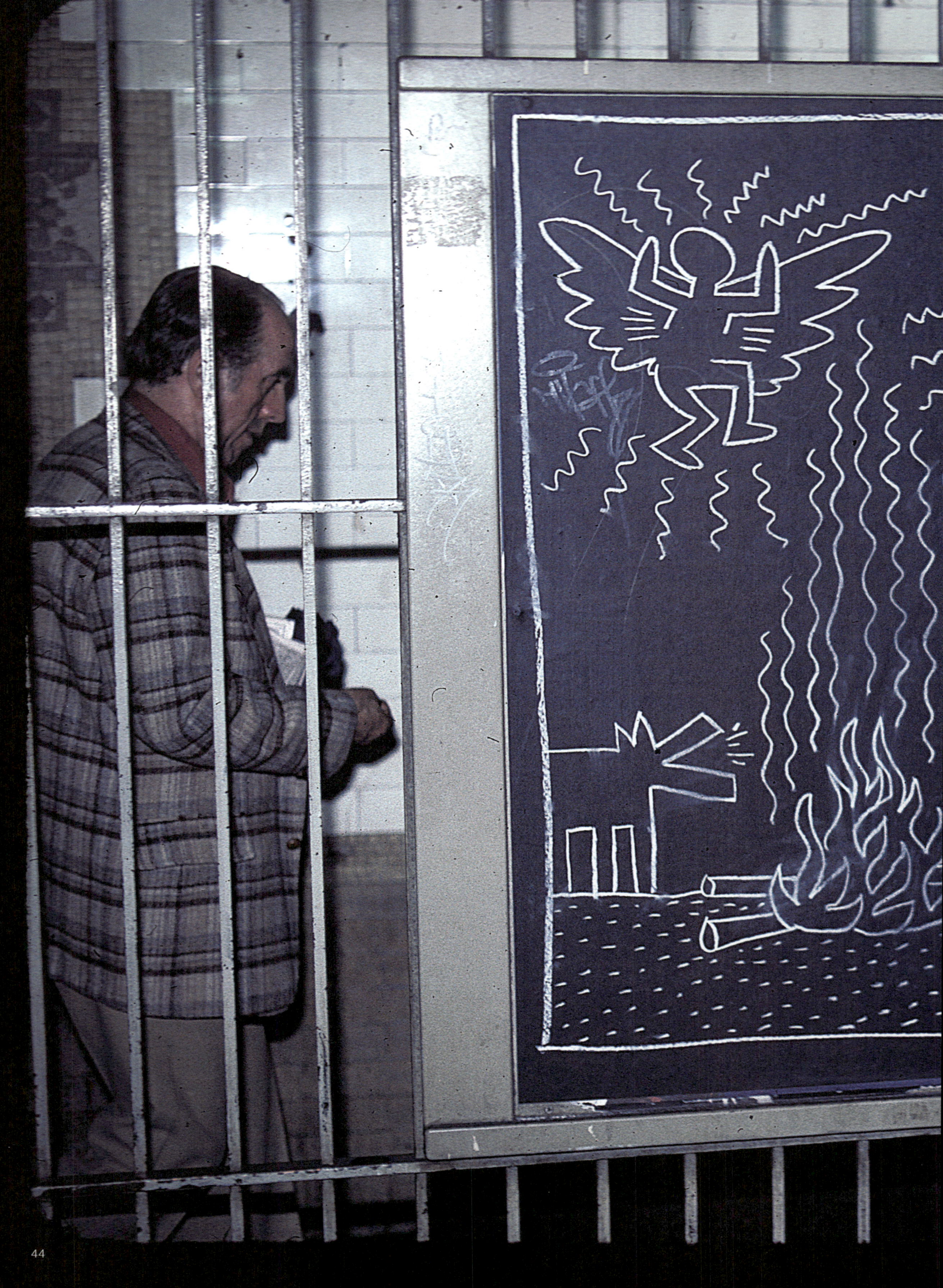

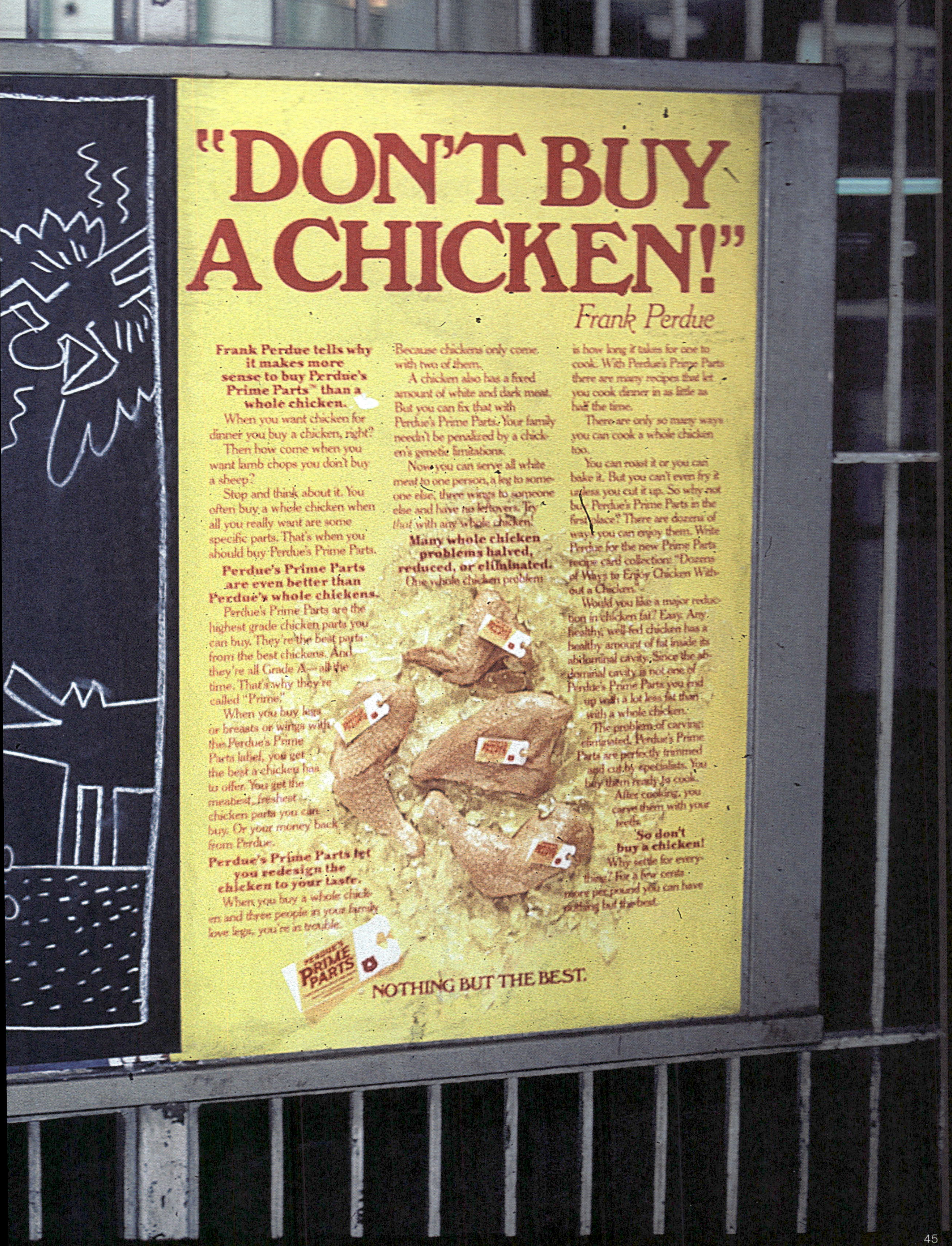

"DON'T BUY A CHICKEN!"
Frank Perdue

Frank Perdue tells why it makes more sense to buy Perdue's Prime Parts™ than a whole chicken.
When you want chicken for dinner you buy a chicken, right?
Then how come when you want lamb chops you don't buy a sheep?
Stop and think about it. You often buy a whole chicken when all you really want are some specific parts. That's when you should buy Perdue's Prime Parts.

Perdue's Prime Parts are even better than Perdue's whole chickens.
Perdue's Prime Parts are the highest grade chicken parts you can buy. They're the best parts from the best chickens. And they're all Grade A—all the time. That's why they're called "Prime."
When you buy legs or breasts or wings with this Perdue's Prime Parts label, you get the best a chicken has to offer. You get the meatiest, freshest chicken parts you can buy. Or your money back from Perdue.

Perdue's Prime Parts let you redesign the chicken to your taste.
When you buy a whole chicken and three people in your family love legs, you're in trouble.

Because chickens only come with two of them.
A chicken also has a fixed amount of white and dark meat. But you can fix that with Perdue's Prime Parts. Your family needn't be penalized by a chicken's genetic limitations.
Now you can serve all white meat to one person, a leg to someone else, three wings to someone else and have no leftovers. Try that with any whole chicken!

Many whole chicken problems halved, reduced, or eliminated.
One whole chicken problem is how long it takes for one to cook. With Perdue's Prime Parts there are many recipes that let you cook dinner in as little as half the time.
There are only so many ways you can cook a whole chicken too.
You can roast it or you can bake it. But you can't even fry it unless you cut it up. So why not buy Perdue's Prime Parts in the first place? There are dozens of ways you can enjoy them. Write Perdue for the new Prime Parts recipe card collection: "Dozens of Ways to Enjoy Chicken Without a Chicken."
Would you like a major reduction in chicken fat? Easy. Any healthy, well-fed chicken has a healthy amount of fat inside its abdominal cavity. Since the abdominal cavity is not one of Perdue's Prime Parts you end up with a lot less fat than with a whole chicken.
The problem of carving eliminated. Perdue's Prime Parts are perfectly trimmed and cut by specialists. You buy them ready to cook. After cooking, you carve them with your teeth.

So don't buy a chicken!
Why settle for everything? For a few cents more per pound you can have nothing but the best.

PERDUE'S PRIME PARTS

NOTHING BUT THE BEST.

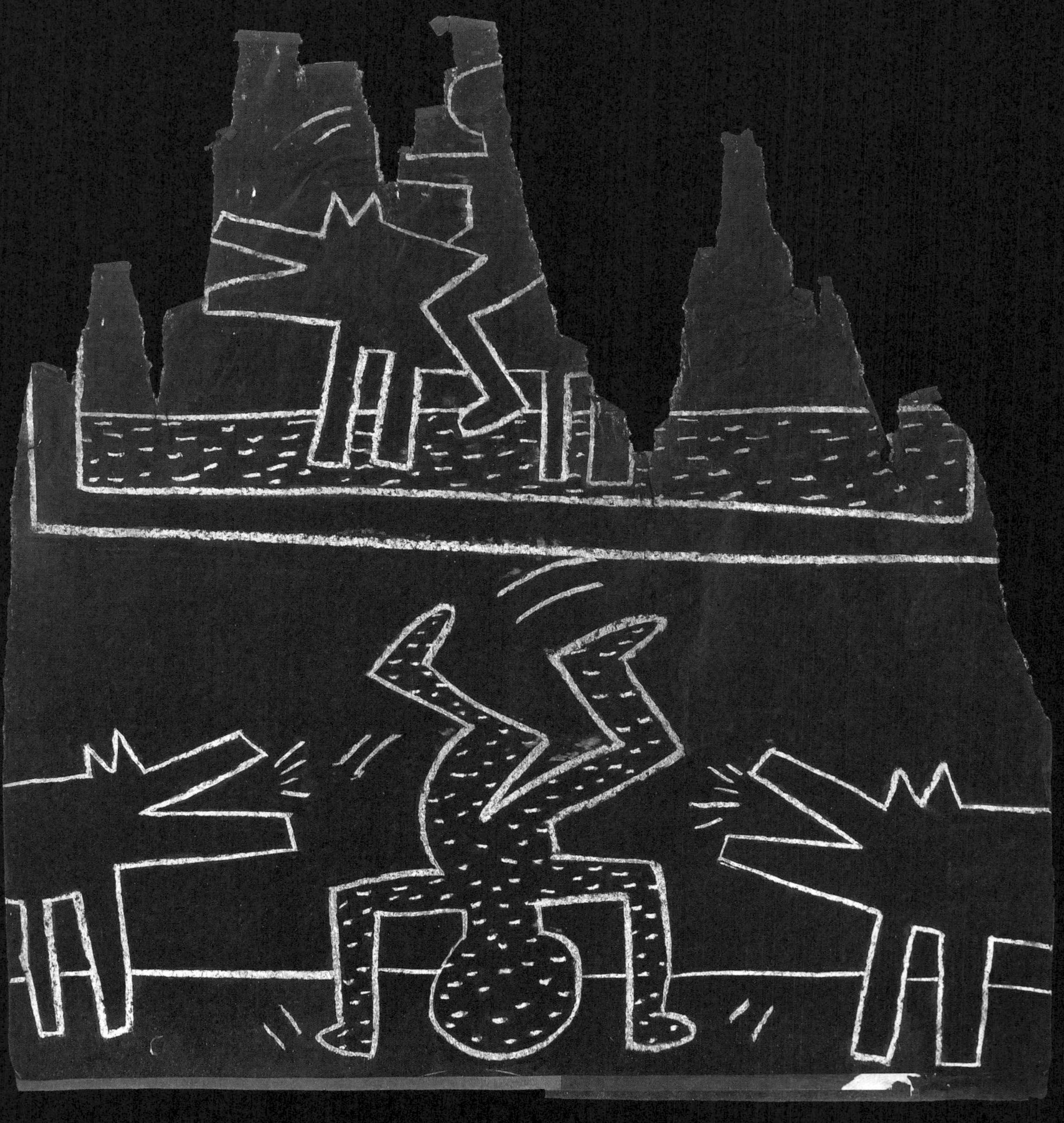

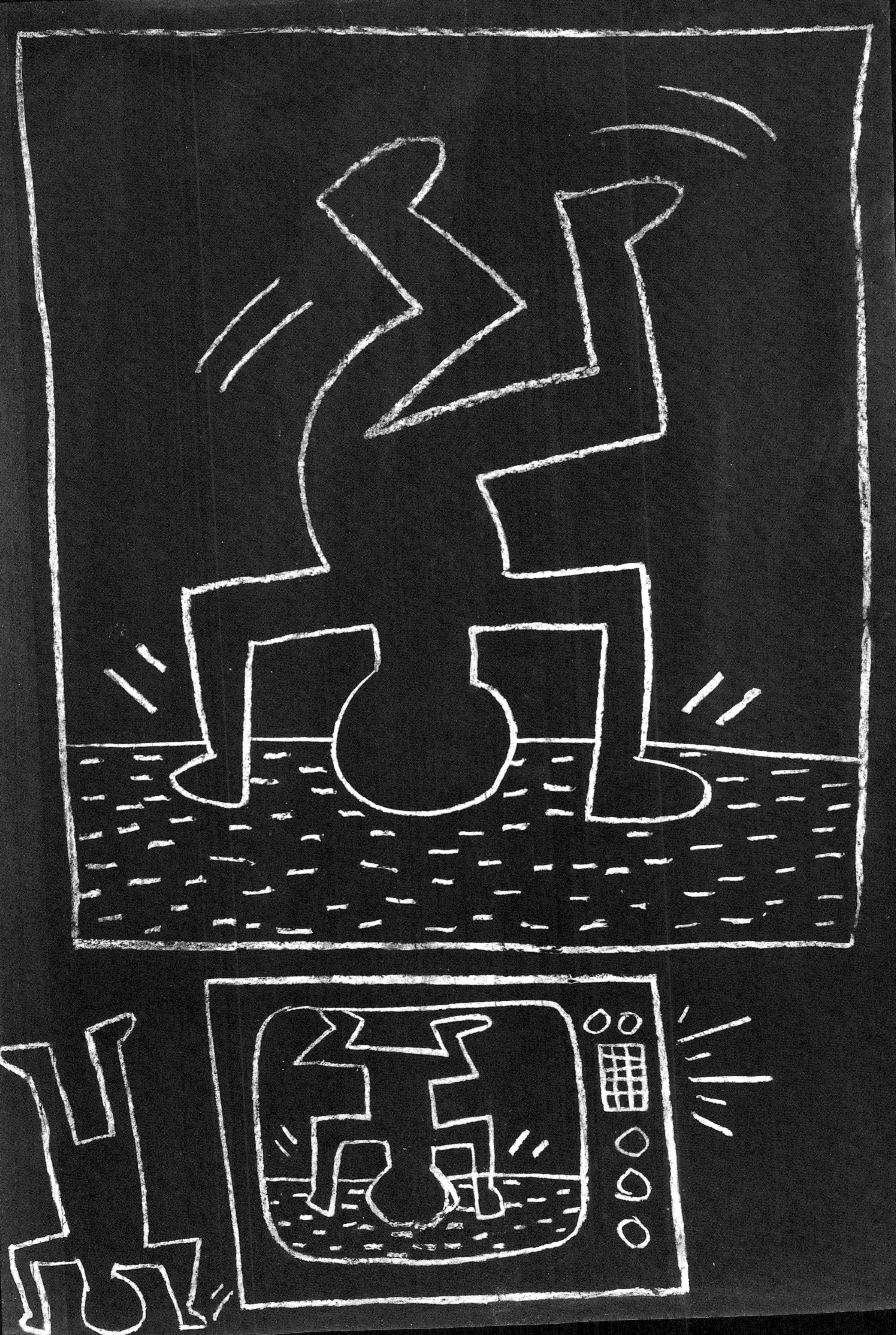

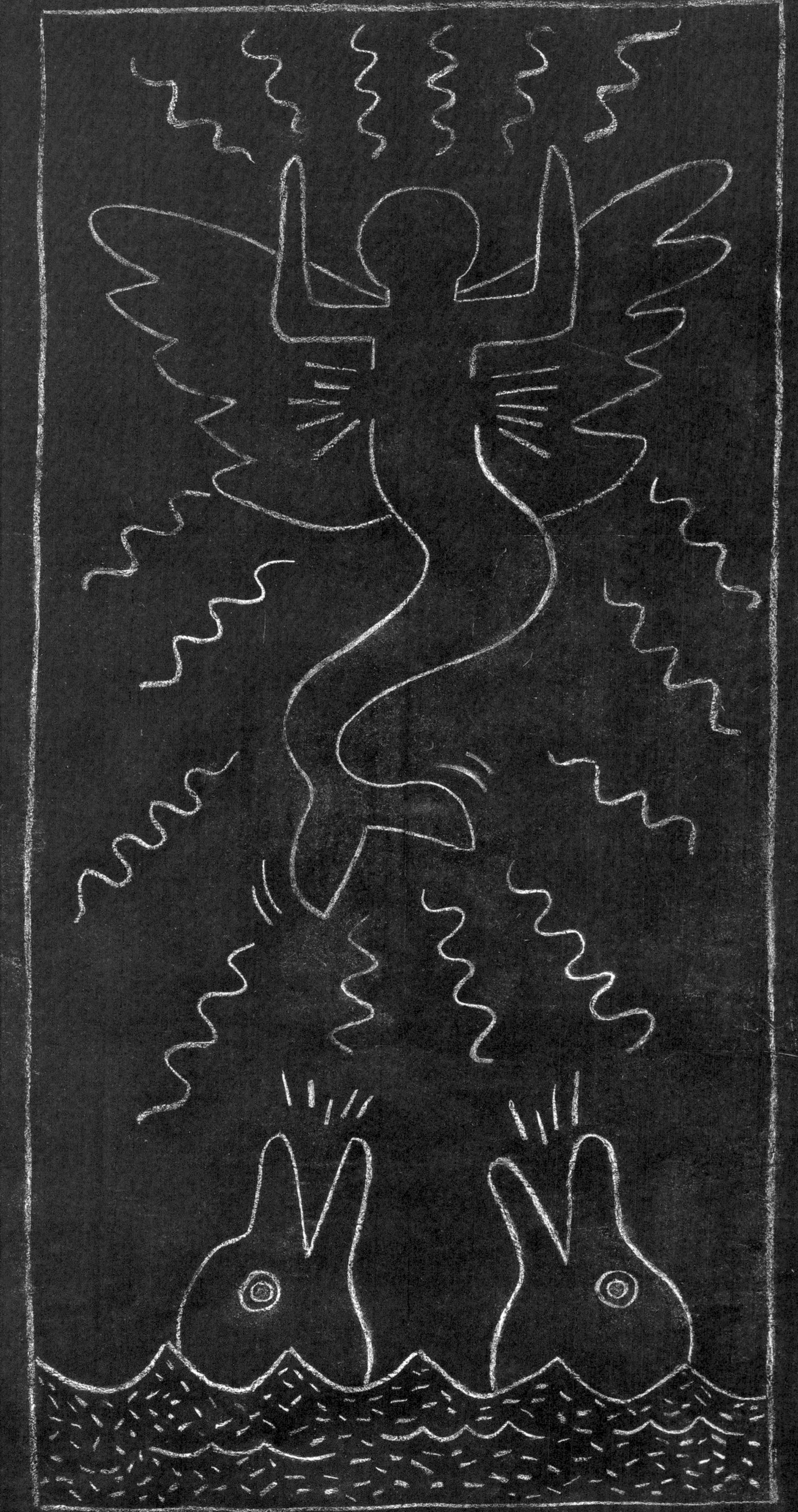

Mass Transit:
Transformation and Transcendence in Keith Haring's Subway Drawings

Carlo McCormick

In one of the most epic conquests of public space ever ventured, over a five-year period Keith Haring produced a titanic, muscular, and mesmerizing body of work across the New York City subway system. To this day, some thirty years after the fact, it remains dauntingly singular in both its scale and its impact upon public consciousness. Dedicated as much to the countless people who might randomly encounter them as to the evanescent present tense to which their most momentary of lives were tethered, Haring's drawings now exist in the posterity of myth and the salvaged shards of urban artifacts, like the impossible relics of some divinely doomed civilization. Because they were not meant to last — briefly inhabiting their temporary lodgings in blacked-out advertising vacancies like itinerant dreams, before being covered up by commerce or torn down by authorities and admirers alike — what little remains of this massive body of work is now oddly esoteric and rarified. And no two terms could be more ill-fitting to this most populist of artists.

A true child of Pop — both as an artist deeply influenced by the Pop Art movement (in particular Warhol) and as an adoring fan of popular culture — Keith Haring always meant his work to be as accessible and comprehensible as possible to the non-art-world public. Indeed, his art remains eminently readable and friendly to those who are not otherwise versed in the privileged discourse of art history and contemporary aesthetics. What has changed, and become a bit more obscure, is the context surrounding his art. Remarkably fresh and relevant as his imagery and implicit narratives may still be, at this point much else has radically changed. Keith was most insistent that his work be totally open-ended and available to personal interpretation, and that rather than telling people what to think or feel he would provoke them in such a way that they could think for themselves and access their own feelings. With this in mind, it is hardly our place to put much of a specific interpretation into the reader's mind. But perhaps, if we can summon up a sense of the artist, the times, the set and setting for this work — in short, grant these drawings some of their original context, lost in the transposition from their former unsanctioned existence in the less friendly environs of early 1980s New York subway stations to their now ratified place in museums, books, and history — we might just understand them more fully.

As he found and developed his creative voice, a great part of Haring's visual ingenuity sprang from his uncanny ingenuousness. It is often said that all children are great artists, and as such, it is duly noted (to paraphrase Picasso) that for artists to be great they must in some crucial way remain children. Keith Haring certainly brought a measure of that open-eyed wonder and honesty to his artistic expression, conjuring a determined innocence and steadfast love for humanity as his work came to confront and question the most problematic aspects of the human condition. While this emphatic positivism is surely his own and fully endemic to his character, we must also attribute much of the style and substance by which he conveyed this emotional purity to the vernaculars he adapted as an artist. Primary in this, as both a key element in his art and a matter of biographical fact, was the love for art he found as a child making drawings with his father. These cartoons would continue through his juvenilia; he was inspired by the facility of this form in communicating with people. It would misdirect him, briefly, toward pursuing a commercial art degree for illustration, and — by the time he came to New York City in 1978 to study at the School of Visual Arts (SVA) — it would commingle with an assortment of other visual strategies and tropes to evolve within, but never fully leave, his creative practice.

The cartoon-comic sensibility is evident in the entirety of Keith Haring's subway drawings, particularly in the deft personifications by which he anthropomorphizes many central elements in his iconography (such as the barking dogs, robots, snakes and dolphins) giving them added metaphorical resonance as symbolic societal stand-ins. But that sensibility is perhaps less obviously central to the sense of dramatic narrative that these pictures convey. We read them as pictures — and remember here that our ability to read them was of paramount importance to Keith — because they follow a common language established by comics for over a century. They remain incidents, for they are of course just single images. But the implication is that they are single panels from a vast serial strip, their comic language implying the precedence and consequence to the incident before us. Without the linguistic cacophony of word balloons, sequential illustrations, or other tropes typical of the comic medium, Haring conveys this sense of unfolding story most subtly: by drawing a line around the border of each of his drawings, creating a frame within

the frame of the work it-
self, thus mimicking the
grid of comics.

Of course, this frame
that Haring creates around
the drawing, gratuitous to
the composition but fun-
damental to its mediation,
is also evocative of the
television screen, which
would certainly rank high
in his populist pantheon. In this we
might be reminded of the cultural
war that has raged across genera-
tions over the detrimental effects of
children's amusements. Long before
parents would come to blame the
antisocial values of rock music, sexuality on television, or violence in vid-
eo games, the first real shot in these
culture wars was in fact fired against
comics — espoused by one of those
self-serving moralists, by the name
of Frederic Wertham, in his alarmist
screed *Seduction of the Innocent*.
Published in 1954, it created a
McCarthy-era climate of recrimina-
tions, industry self-censorship, and
a reduction to puerile pabulum that
would eventually culminate in the
birth of the underground comics that
would have a tremendous influence
on Haring and his contemporaries
in the graffiti art movement. While
that bit of history is indeed of some
relevance to Haring's development,
we invoke it here to consider more
generally the effects of television on
his generation — in particular, the
consensus view that television was
somehow rotting the mind of kids. Of
course, there is a sharpness of wit
and insight in Haring's art that would
belie all such claims, but in his radically reductive, careening narratives,
his emphatic flattening of space,
and his propensity towards magical
thinking, we must also acknowledge
the immense power that the televis-
ual experience had on toddlers like
him, who grew up in front of the television screen throughout the 1960s.
The genius here, in how we relate to
it, is that of an idiot-box-savant.

It is no wonder that Haring, in
seeking a universal language, would
appropriate the figurative iconography of cartoon art. But immersed in

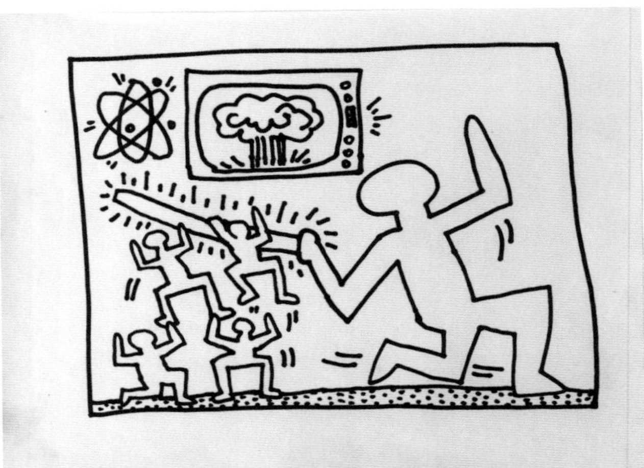

the cultural milieu of New York City,
his exposure to a broader canon of
aesthetic precedents would ensure
that he was far more than a cartoon
artist. It's always perilous to presume
too much about an artist's creative
diet, but among those influences
that Keith personally acknowledged
and that left a clear mark on his art,
we must note the linearity of calligraphy, the gestures of painting (perhaps, in the spontaneity with which
he worked, most closely related to
action painting), the study of semiotics that would help formulate the
iconic signs of his pictographic language, and the process-based aspects of performance and concep-
tual art. Diverse though they may
be as a set of influences, their most
relevant commonality is that, as a
matter of expression, all of them em-
body a primacy and simplicity that
remains at the heart of what is so
appealing in Haring's art.

For all that Keith Haring learned
and adapted from fine art and popular culture, no greater creative debt,
inspiration, or germinal impulse can
be seen in his art than the graffiti renaissance that was occurring in
New York City when he arrived here.
Keith was quite forthcoming about
how seeing graffiti work on the trains
influenced, prompted, and stimu-
lated his drawings on the blacked-
out subway advertising spaces. He
was just as clear that what he himself was doing was not graffiti. This
is a crucial distinction, and one that
is a lot easier to make today than it
was when Haring was working underground. Though he was in many
ways singular as an artist, the truth
is that however unique his interpretation of graffiti's sensibilities may
have been, among New York artists

he was hardly alone
in the way graffiti ig-
nited his creativity and
the intentions it engen-
dered. Inspired by graf-
fiti's scale, style, linguistic play, visual eye-candy
appeal, and immediate
access to a culturally diverse, non-art-world au-
dience, Haring was one
of many who followed the pictorial
strategies of the movement. In fact,
by the time he began his own con-
quest of the subway system, the entire downtown art scene to which he
belonged was pretty much intoxicat-
ed by the allure of aerosol art.

Among the other artists who extended their studio practices to begin working in non-commissioned,
often illegal ways on the urban canvas during the late 1970s and early
1980s, were John Ahearn, John
Fekner, Richard Hambleton, David
Hammonds, Jenny Holzer, Barbara
Kruger, Tom Otterness, Dan Witz,
David Wojnarowicz, as well as two
of Keith's friends, Kenny Scharf and
Jean-Michel Basquiat. As socially
comingled as the scenes were then
— especially with a generation of
masters from the trains, like Crash,
Daze, Fab 5 Freddy, Futura 2000,
Lee Quinones and Dondi White hitting a level of aesthetic aspiration
that would take their work to canvas—there was a time when the
separation of these otherwise diver-
gent genres seemed specious, the
sense of overriding community rein-
forced by the fact the artists would
often exhibit and hang together in
the same nightclubs, galleries, and
alternative spaces like Mudd Club,
Fun Gallery, and Fashion Moda,
and at events like the seminal Times
Square Show of 1980. Ultimately,
most understood that what Haring
and the aforementioned artists were
doing was not graffiti, and it is only
in retrospect, with the emergence
of artists like Shepard Fairey and
Banksy, that we can understand this
particular phenomenon as the nas-
cent gestures of street art.

Even within this retrospective
understanding of street art, there

are some salient aspects of what Haring was doing that make his work conspicuously different from what many of his peers were up to. Most obvious are scale and visibility; as prolific as many artists may have been in their street work then, none came close to Keith's immense output. Identity branding through the massive saturation of one's regional topography with a tag (in Haring's case interestingly, the antithesis of a tag, as he never signed his "public" art) was a lesson Haring learned well from graffiti, and part of his considerable legacy to street art today. As well, there is a marked difference in the tone and content of Haring's expression as opposed to that of many others working on the street, who approached the genre with more political agendas. Keith's was a socially engaged work, frequently alluding to global events and dealing with a number of ideologically loaded issues that were part of the collective conscious, such as our general dis-ease in relation to technology, Cold War antagonisms, and conflicted ideas regarding God and evolution. But it remained remarkably devoid of the polemical didactics inherent to political art. Always implicit in this work was an abiding trust that people would bring their own viewpoints and could come to their own conclusions, and that as far apart as we may be in our subjective understanding of reality, we are always bound together in our common anxieties and capacity for faith.

A more tantalizing distinguishing characteristic of Haring's oeuvre is his choice of medium. If we begin by considering his "canvas," the decision to commandeer ad space is inherently provocative. While he only occasionally referenced nearby advertising his drawings, more often responding only to the blank of the absent ad, the fact that he did address advertisements is not accidental. Far less known among Haring's street art are the Xeroxed posters he made from

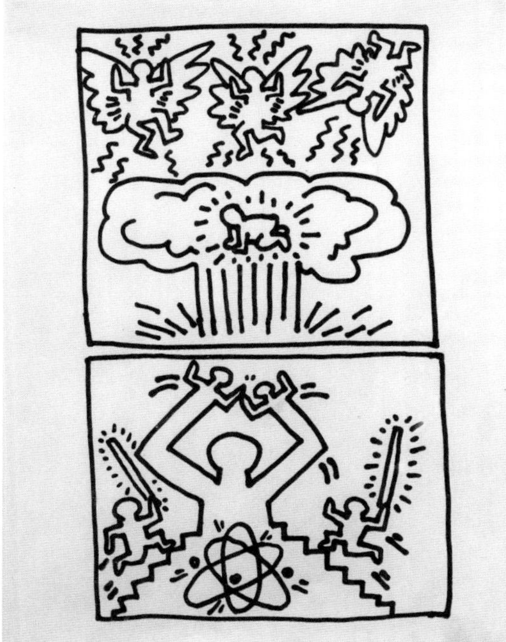

cut-up tabloid newspapers and wheat-pasted to city walls. In this coincident tendency we see more clearly how acutely attuned Haring was to a number of cultural tendencies, including William S. Burroughs and Brion Gysin's post-automatic-writing cut-up strategies, Punk's DIY ethos of creating one's own media, the emergence of a new post-modernist attitude towards art (which often used appropriation and advertising techniques), and the Situationist practice of *detournement*, or altering the meaning of a work — notably advertising or billboards — to contradict its original intention. This practice, it must be said, extended the Situationist legacy from the late 1960s through a wide range of public-art-based cultural critiques, from the Billboard Liberation Front that began in the late 1970s through Adbusters and the current Occupy movement, and it is endemic to the very raison d'être of contemporary street art.

In addition to referencing advertising, the other notable feature of Haring's medium is his use of chalk. Far more impermanent than the more typical spray paint, chalk embraces its own ephemerality in ways that contradict the quest for immortality so fundamental to the arts. The discrete charm of Haring's choice of material is that, long before the use of markers and spray paints, the earliest graffiti in New York was done by children drawing with chalk on the streets.

Knowing and naïve, erupting out of an urban polyglot as a concise hieroglyphics we could all comprehend, and driven to some impossibly accelerated rate — as if it could keep up with the sheer velocity of the city itself — Keith Haring's art of rapid transit was uncannily as much about its own transitory place in the world as it was about those most uniquely human capacities for transformation and transcendence. Keith was the embodiment of the radiant baby he made famous, and for anyone who encountered his iconic personification of transpersonal purity, indefectible innocence, and implacable honesty, they too would, for some irresistible moment of grace, inherit those attributes themselves. Bringing beauty and a near-blinding ray of hope to the dark and distressing subterranean world of the subway, his art manifested in a universe of strangers the capacity for transmogrification it so poetically illustrated. From his glowing rods, UFOs, orbiting atoms and radiating pyramids to the babies, robots, angels, and praying figures that populated his drawings, Haring illuminated the very energy he was drawing: a power both apocalyptic and rescuing, at once imbued with the destructive capacity and terror of our nuclear age and resonant of a sublime mystical force. And Keith Haring did all this in such short order, in the briefest span of a tragically abridged life. He left behind a stunning autographic pictography that still speaks to us today — never preconceived but always spot on, conjuring a mystery we all could understand with a supremely confident hand. In it we can intuit the authority of an Imagineering animator, the persuasive charm of a slick adman, and the unruly voice of all who are bound by an abiding sense of truth to question the lies of our consensus reality. And yes, it all still shines brightly today. ■

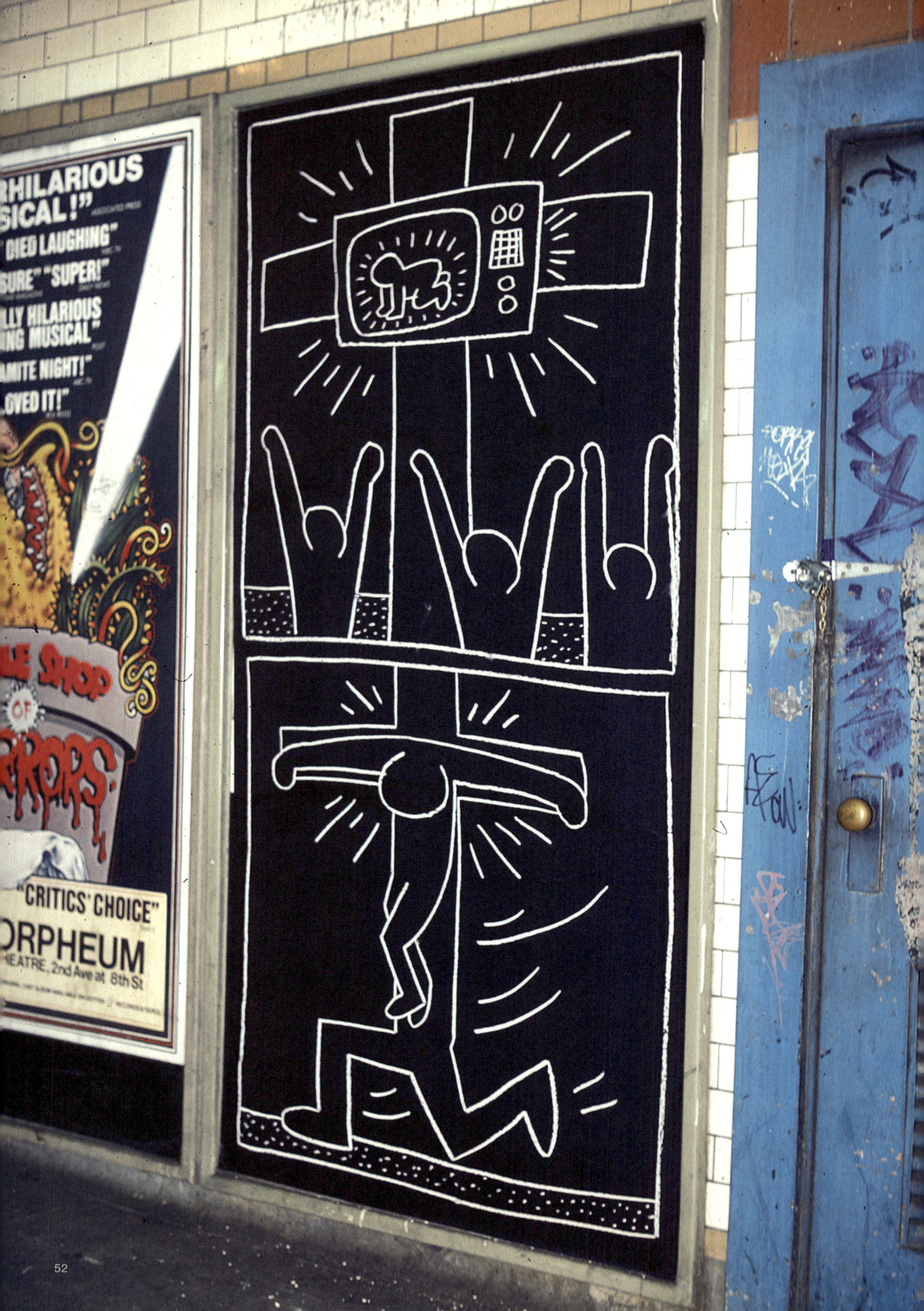

RHILARIOUS
SICAL !"
" DIED LAUGHING"
SURE" "SUPER!"
LLY HILARIOUS
NG MUSICAL"
AMITE NIGHT!"
OVED IT!"
LE SHOP
OF
RRORS
"CRITICS' CHOICE"
ORPHEUM
HEATRE, 2nd Ave at 8th St

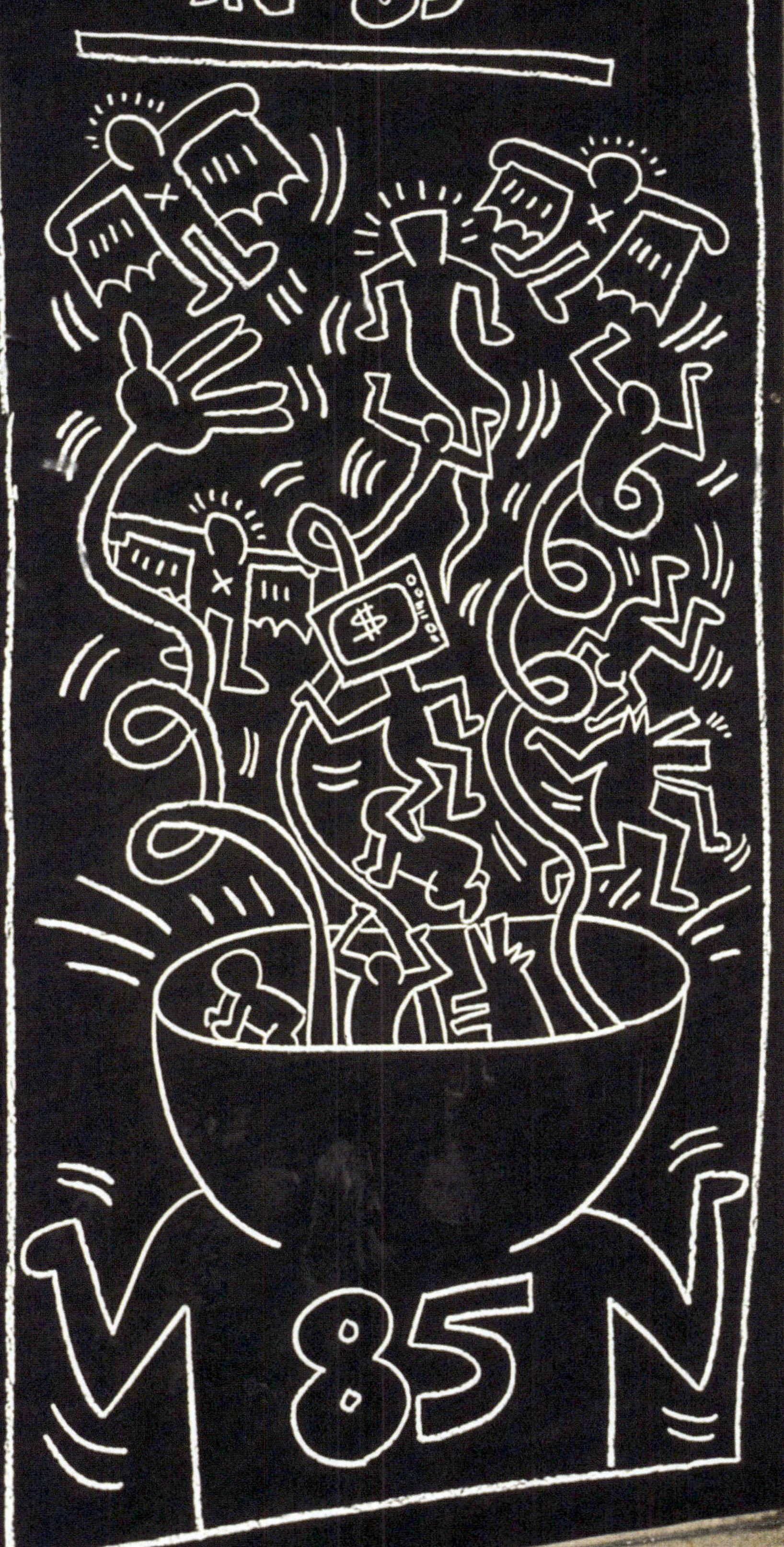
STILL ALIVE
IN 85
$
85

RSC
Royal Shakespeare Company
TWO INTERNATIONALLY ACCLAIMED
PRODUCTIONS IN REPERTORY!
Much Ado About Nothing
by WILLIAM SHAKESPEARE
& Cyrano de Bergerac
HURRY! MUST END JAN. 19th!
LIMITED ENGAGEMENT
DEREK JACOBI
and
SINEAD CUSACK
Gershwin
Theatre
51st St. West of Broadway

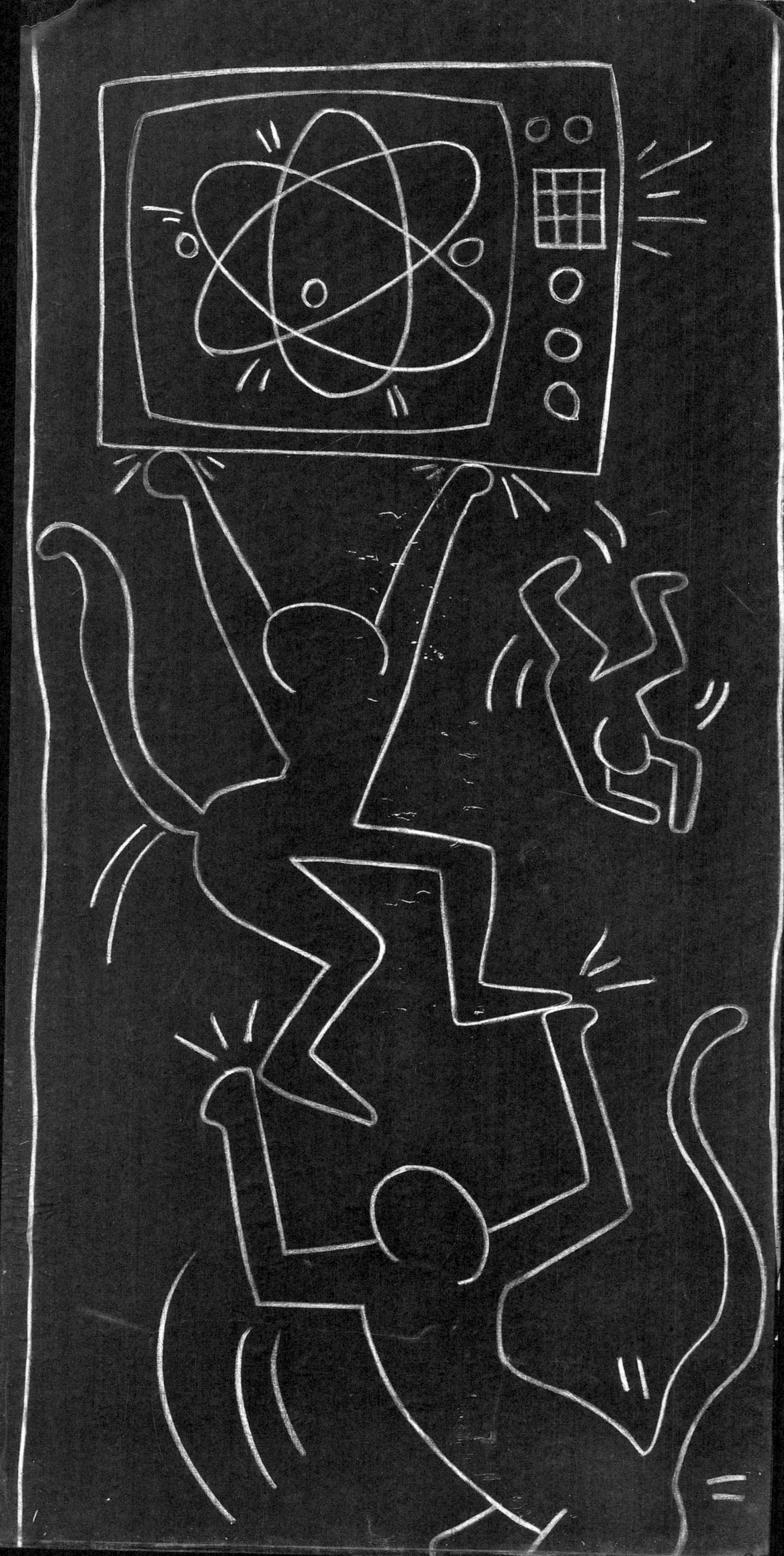

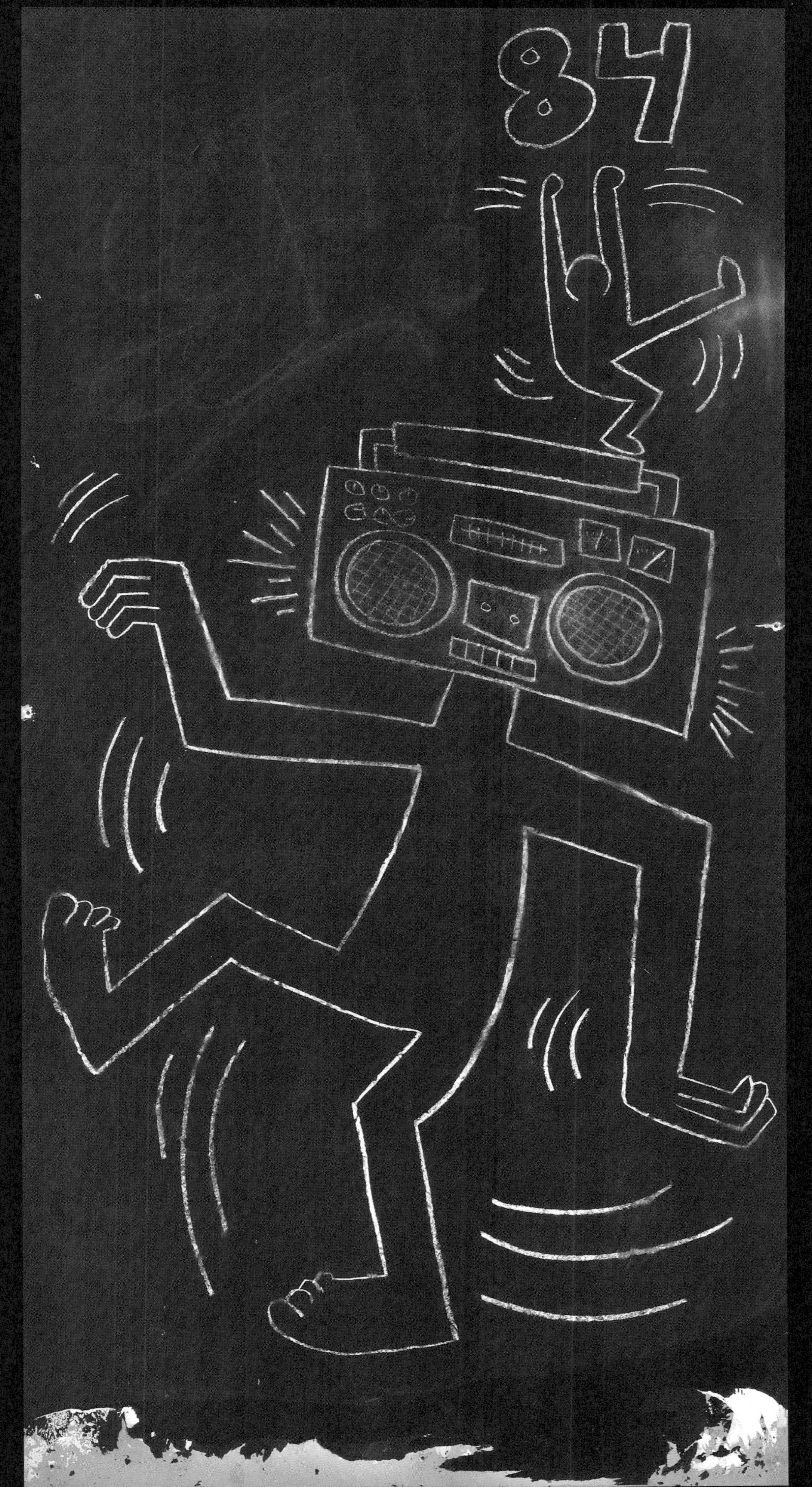
84

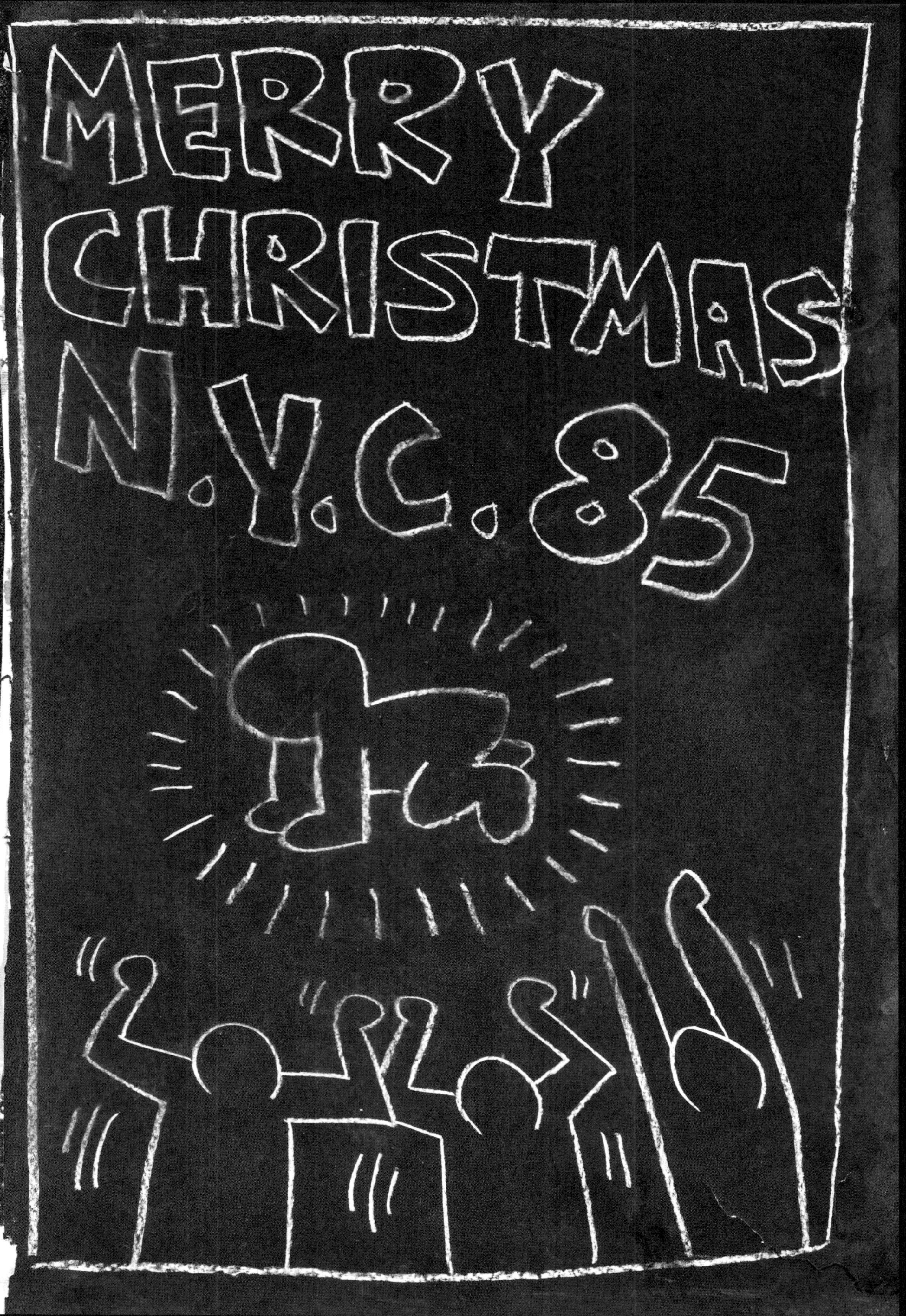

MERRY
CHRISTMAS
N.Y.C. 85

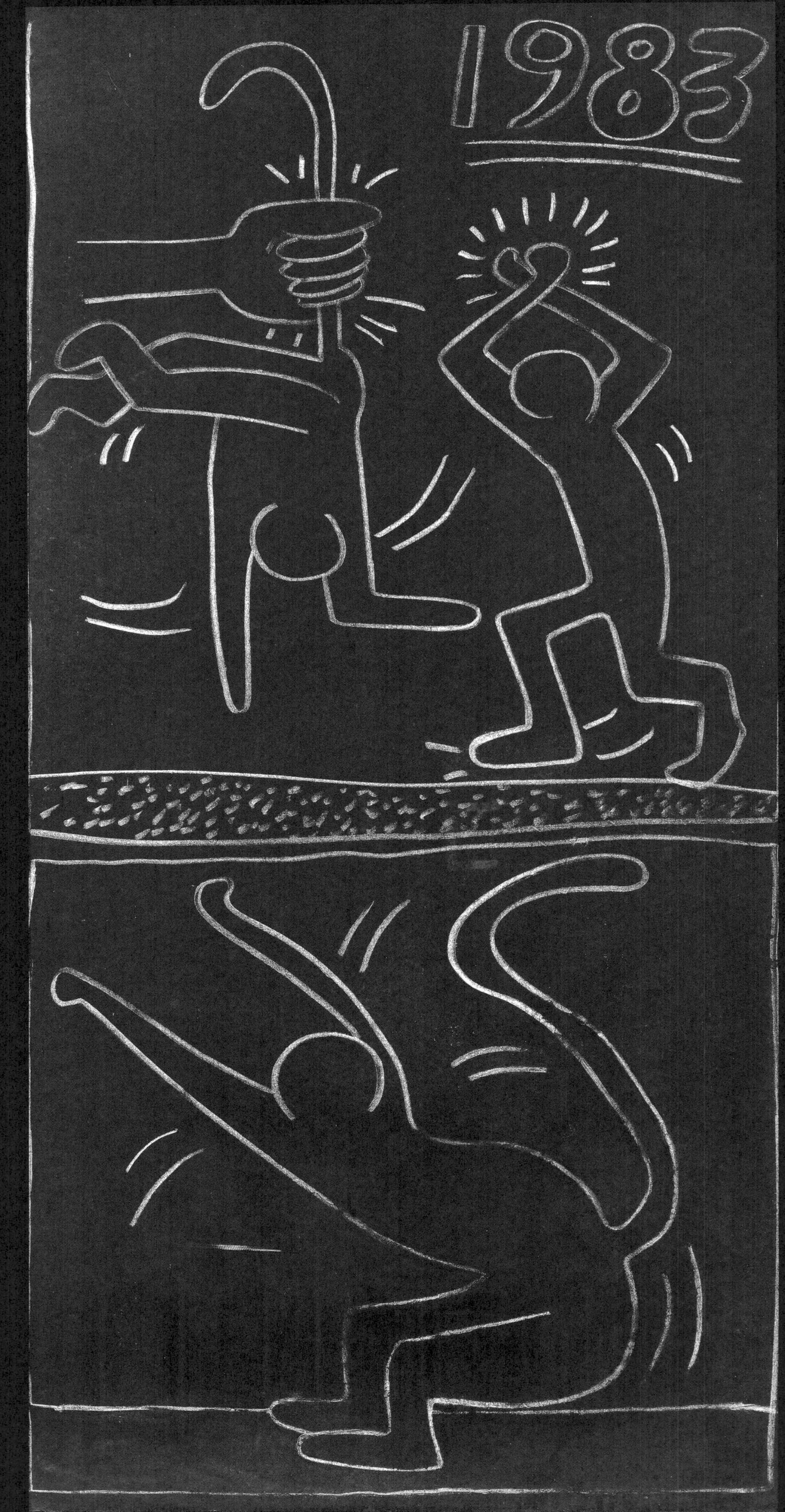
1983

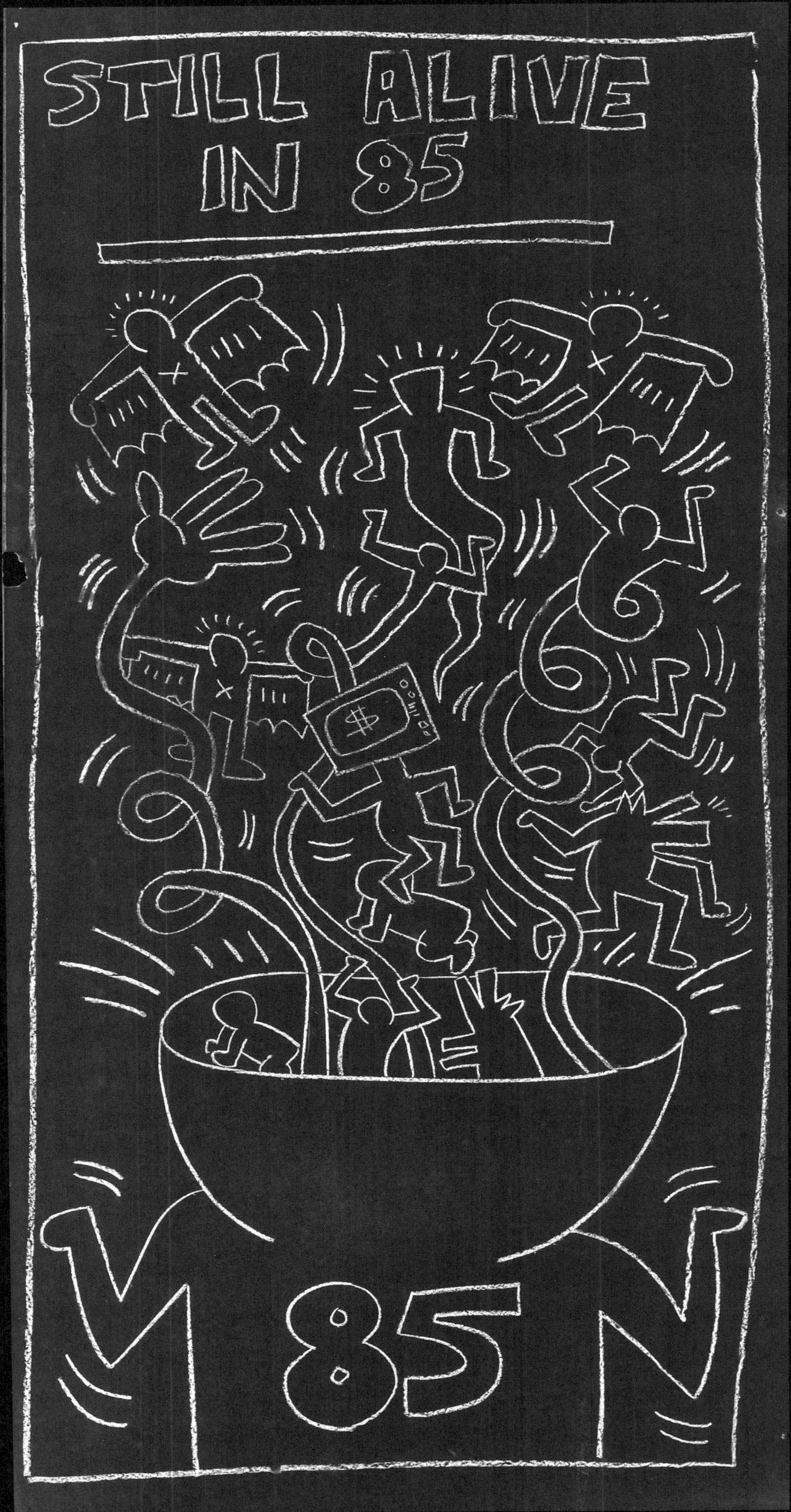

STILL ALIVE
IN 85
85

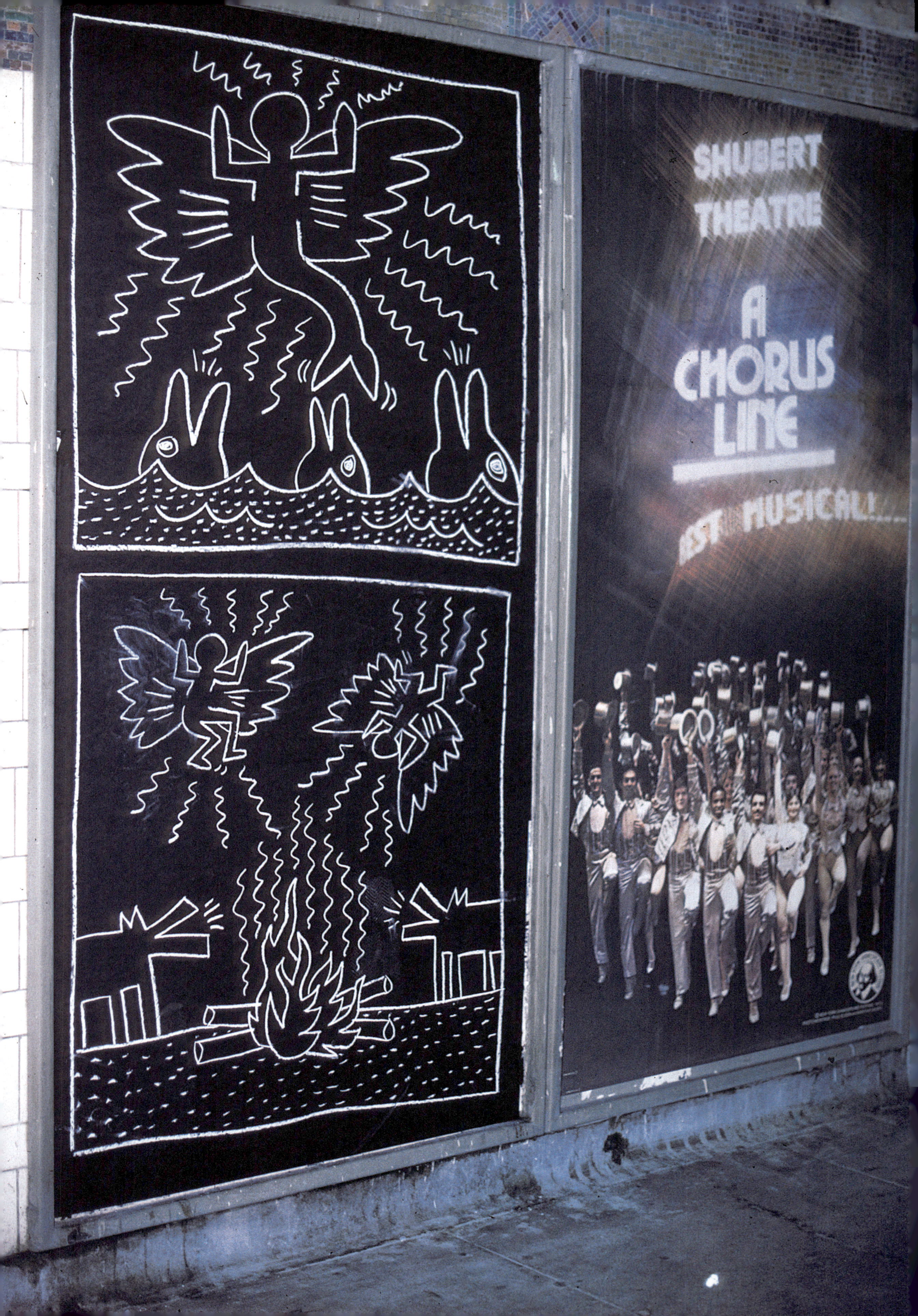

SHUBERT THEATRE
A CHORUS LINE
BEST MUSICAL!

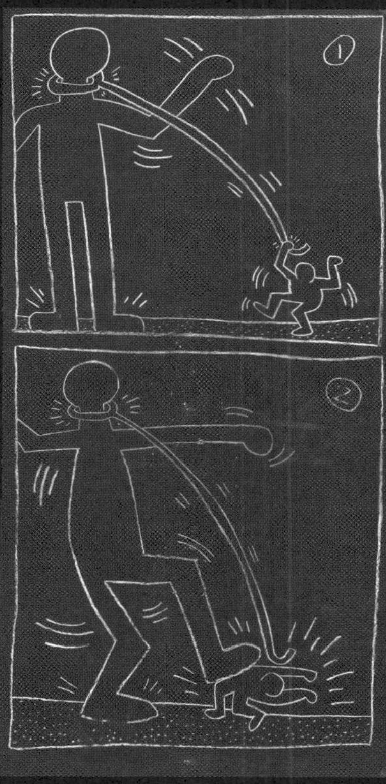

Untitled
Circa 1980 – 1983
Chalk on paper
80 x 45 inches

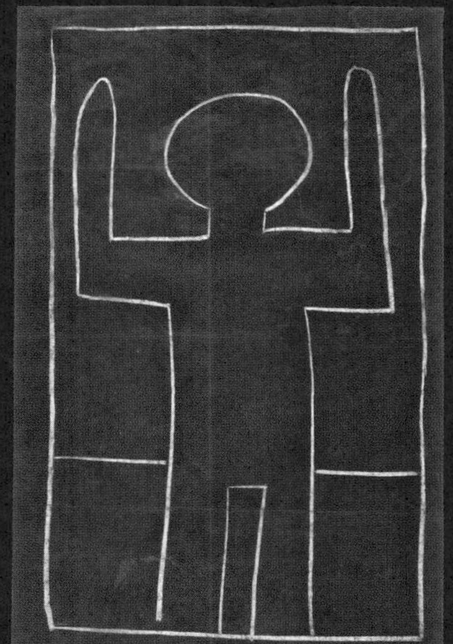

Untitled
Circa 1980 – 1983
Chalk on paper
49 x 32 inches

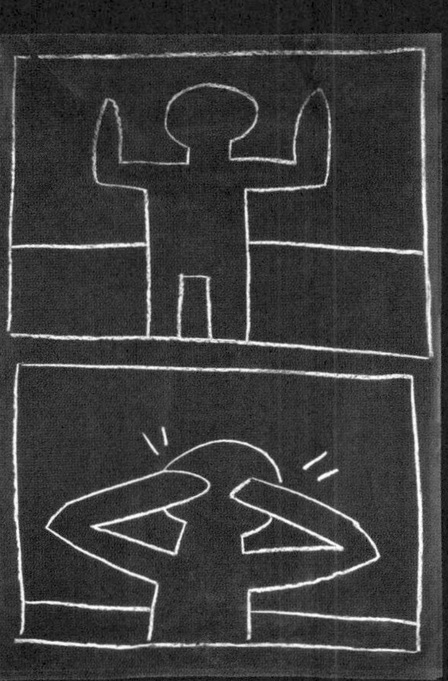

Untitled
Circa 1980 - 1983
Chalk on paper
49 x 34$^{1}/_{4}$ inches

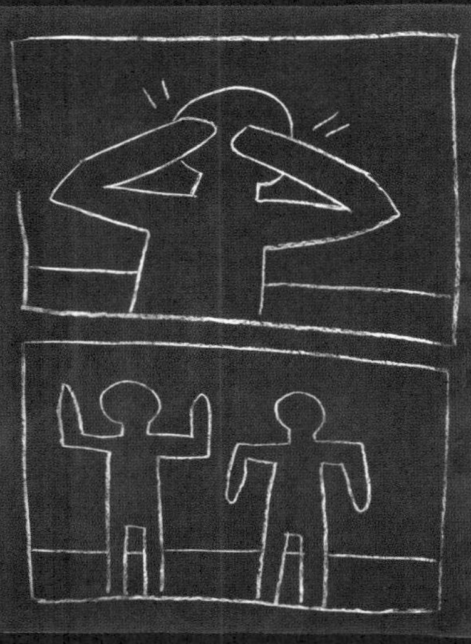

Untitled
Circa 1981-1983
Chalk on paper
49 x 34 inches

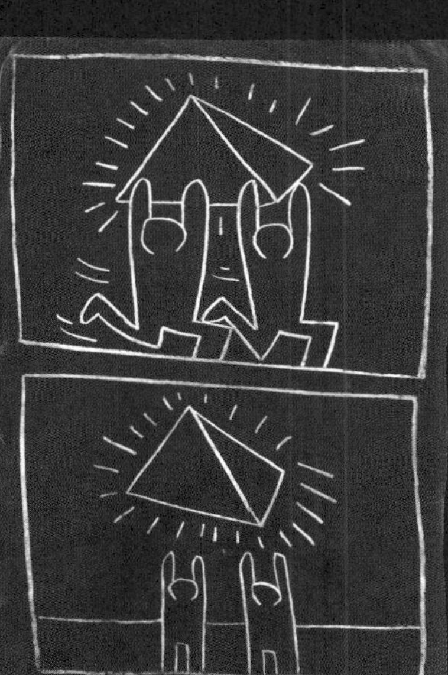

Untitled
Circa 1980 – 1983
Chalk on paper
49 x 34 inches

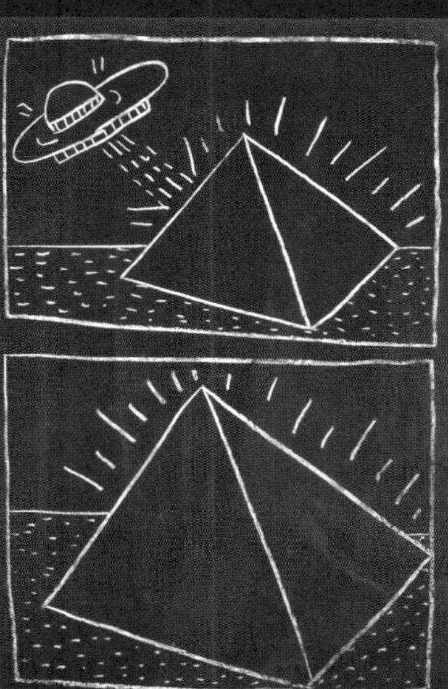

Untitled
Circa 1981-1983
Chalk on paper
49 x 34 inches

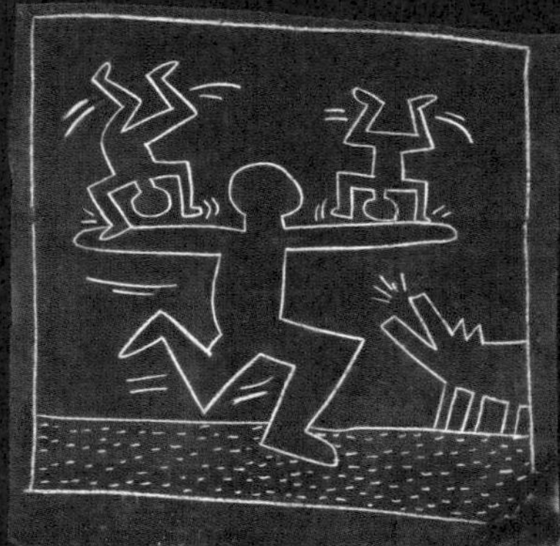

Untitled
Circa 1980 – 1983
Chalk on paper
46 x 45 inches

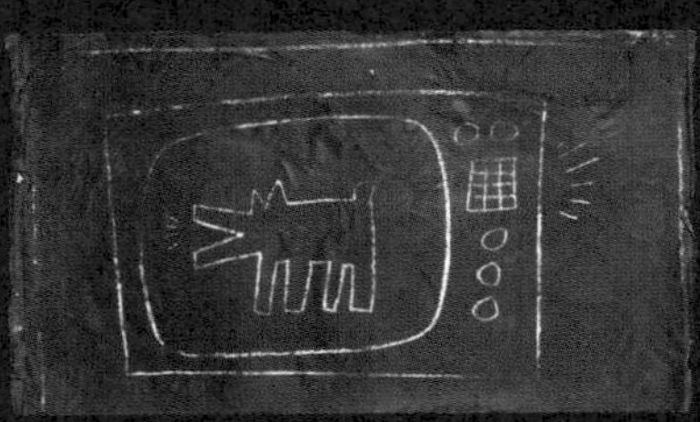

Untitled
Circa 1980 – 1983
Chalk on paper
28 x 45 inches

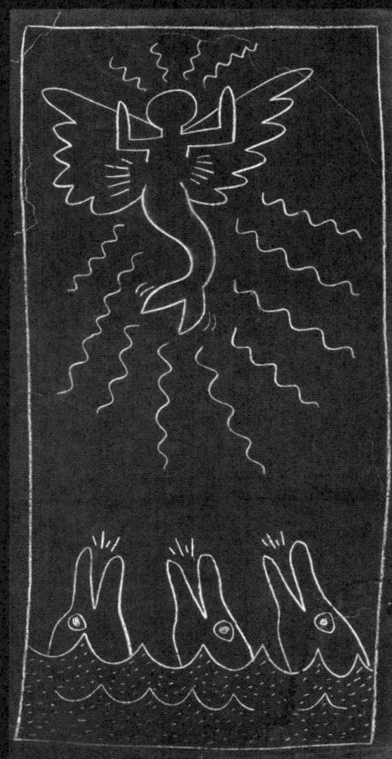

Untitled
1982
Chalk on paper
85 x 43 inches

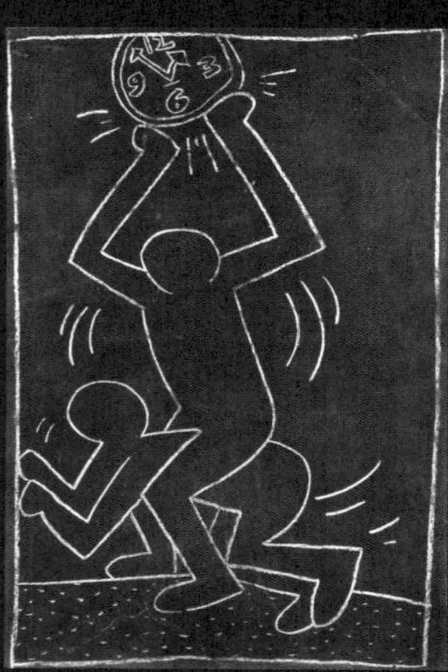

Untitled
Circa 1981 – 1983
Chalk on paper
49 x 34 inches

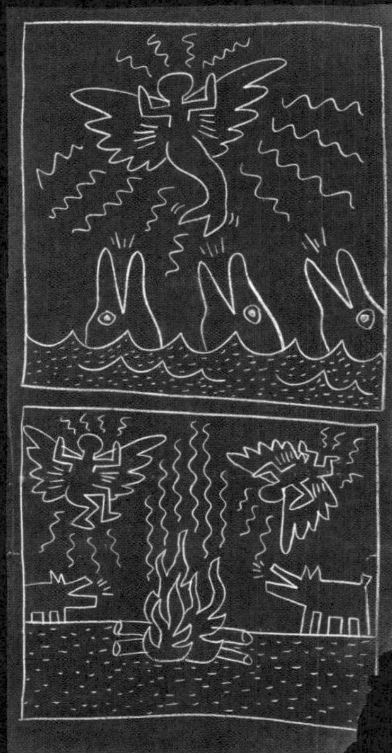

Untitled
Circa 1981 – 1983
Chalk on paper
80 x 45 inches

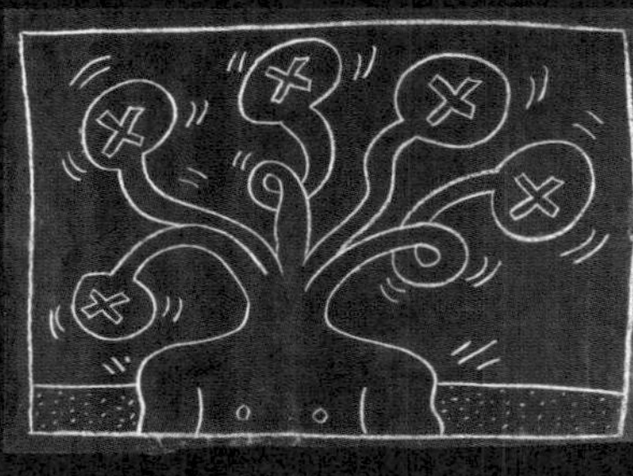

Untitled
Circa 1980 – 1983
Chalk on paper
33¼ x 45¼ inches

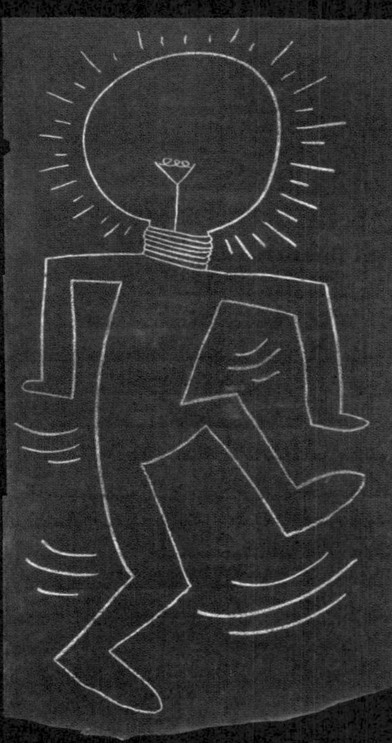

Untitled
Circa 1981 – 1983
Chalk on paper
80 x 45 inches

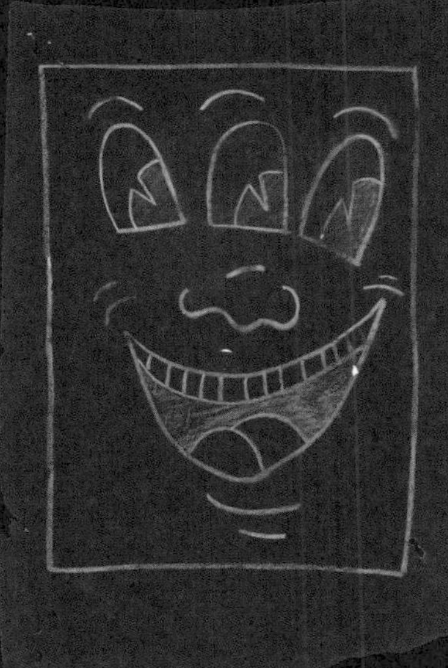

Untitled
Circa 1982 – 1985
Chalk on paper
29 x 22 inches

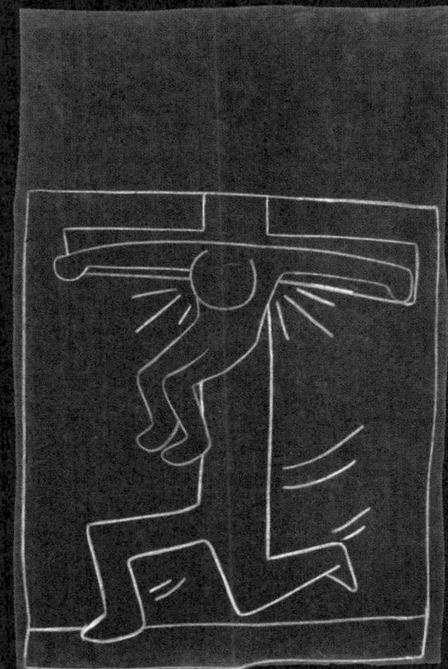

Untitled
Circa 1981 – 1983
Chalk on paper
80 x 45 inches

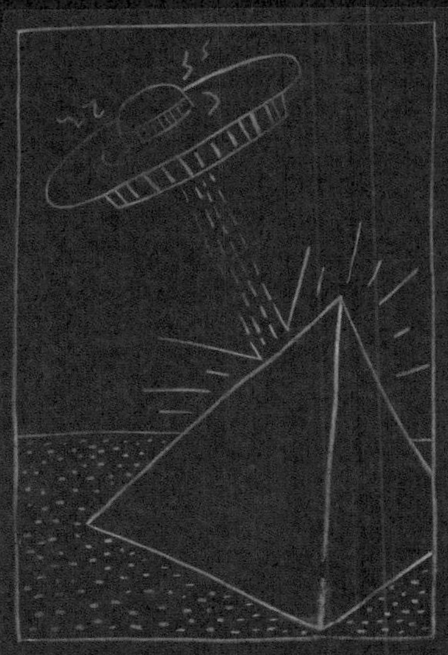

Untitled
Circa 1982 – 1985
Chalk on paper
46 x 29 inches

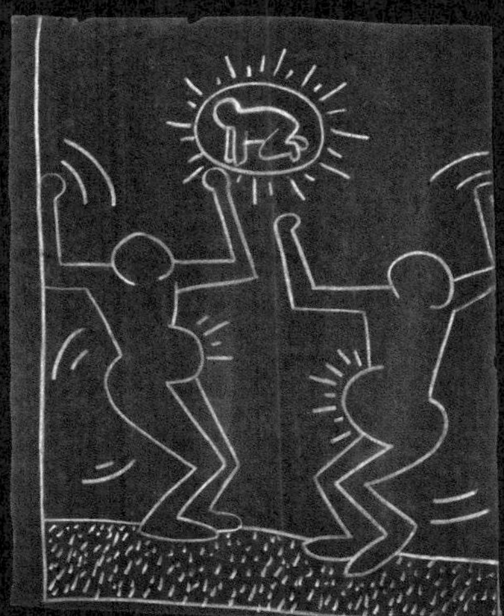

Untitled
Circa 1980 – 1983
Chalk on paper
58 x 46 inches

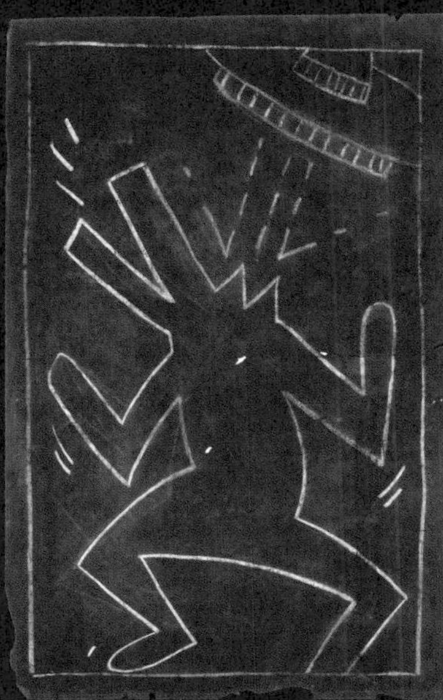

Untitled
Circa 1980 – 1983
Chalk on paper
48³⁄₄ x 32 inches

Untitled
Circa 1980 – 1983
Chalk on paper
48 x 34 inches

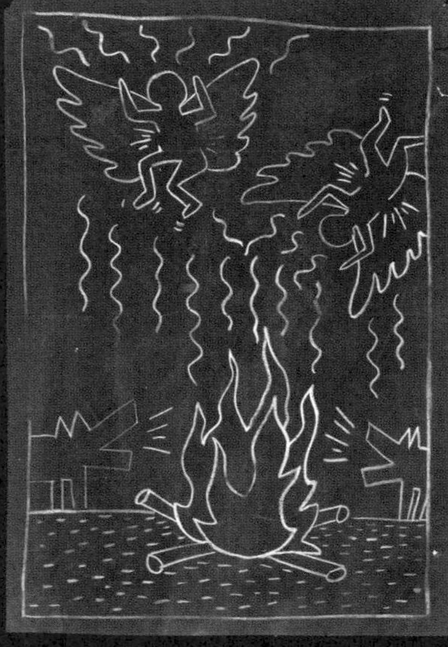

Untitled
Circa 1981 – 1983
Chalk on paper
49 x 34 inches

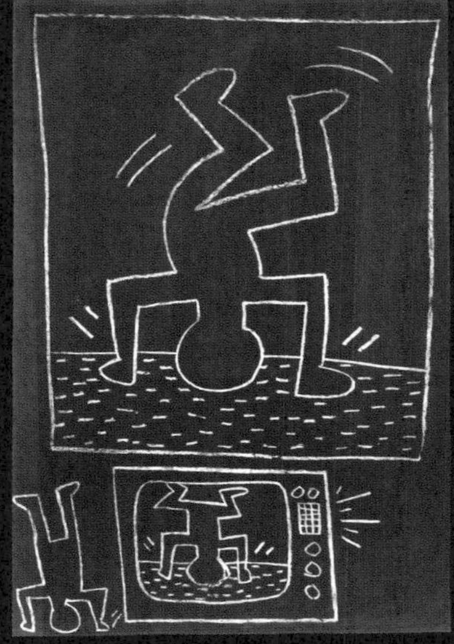

Untitled
Circa 1981-1983
Chalk on paper
49 x 34 inches

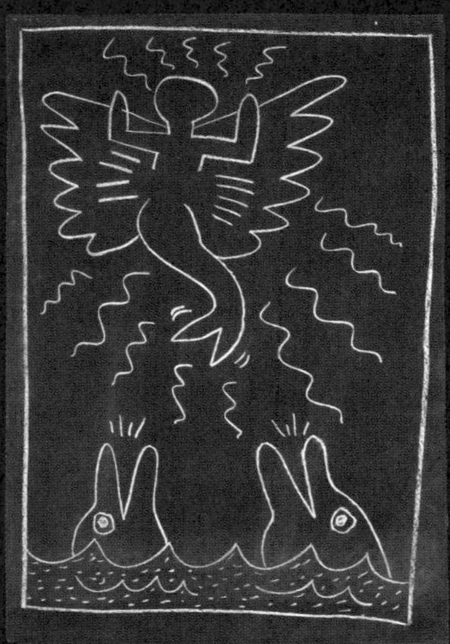

Untitled
Circa 1980 – 1983
Chalk on paper
48¼ x 33¾ inches

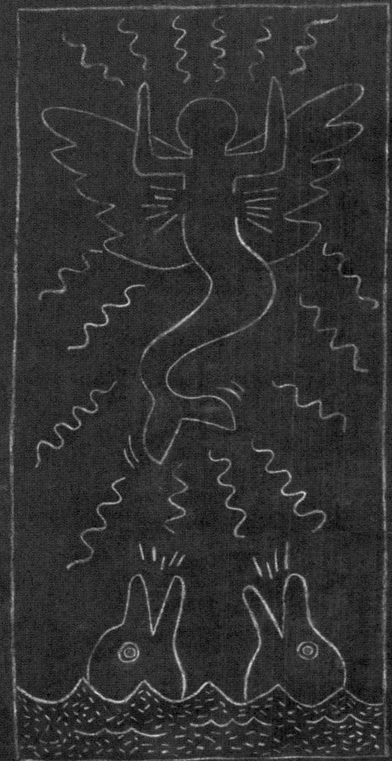

Untitled
Circa 1981 – 1983
Chalk on paper
80 x 45 inches

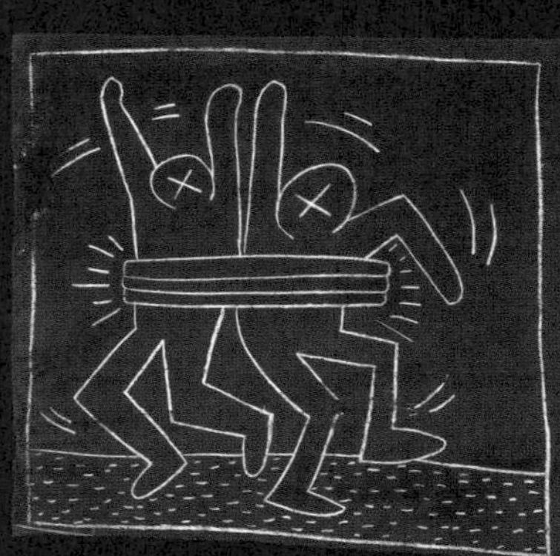

Untitled
Circa 1980 – 1983
Chalk on black paper
43½ x 44¾ inches

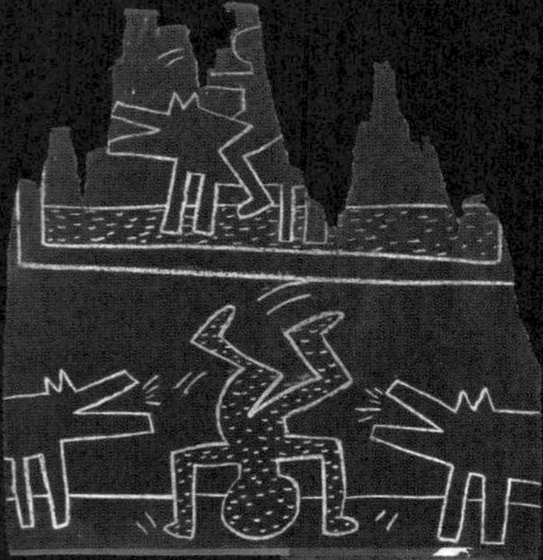

Untitled
Circa 1980 – 1983
Chalk on paper
58 x 46 inches

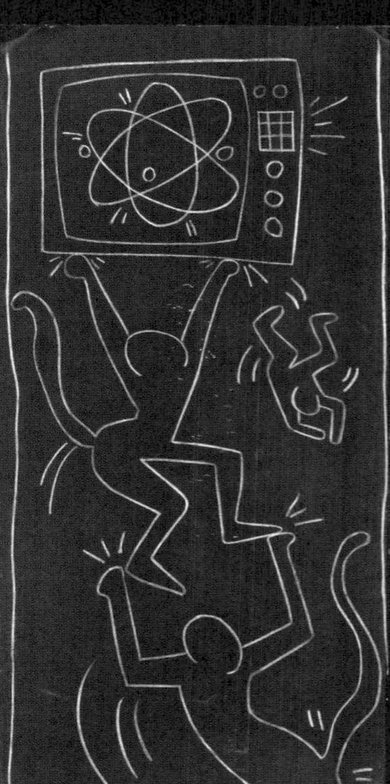

Untitled
1983
Chalk on paper
45 x 58 inches

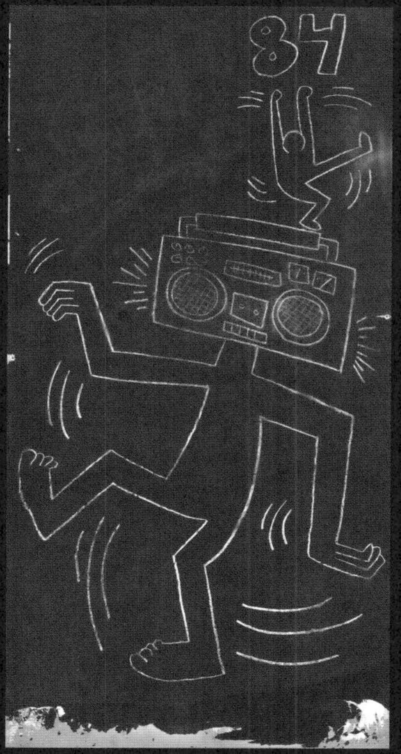

Untitled
1984
Chalk on paper
85½ x 43½ inches

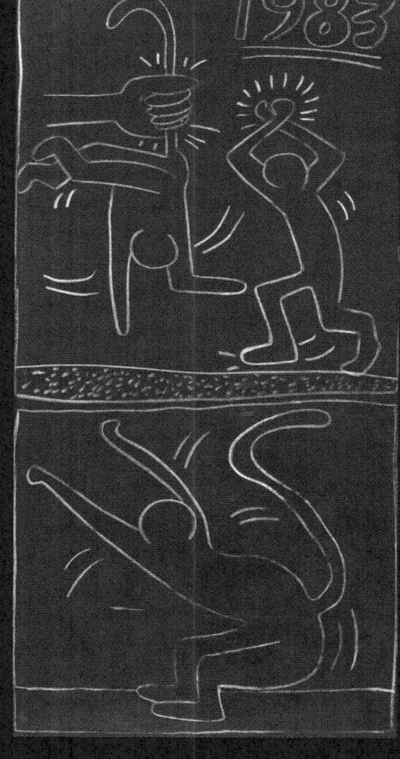

Untitled
1983
Chalk on paper
80 x 45 inches

Untitled
Circa 1980 – 1983
Chalk on paper
34½ x 45 inches

Untitled
1985
Chalk on paper
49 x 45 inches

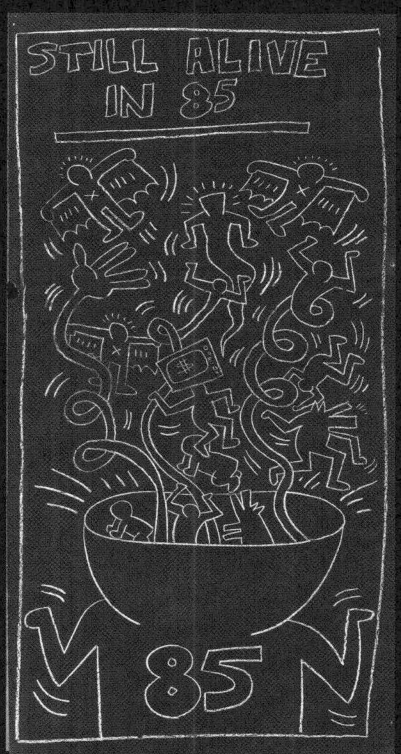

Untitled
1985
Chalk on paper
83 x 41 inches

Contributors

Jeffrey Deitch is director of the Los Angeles Museum of Contemporary Art. Active as an art critic and exhibition curator since the 1970s, he has also served as an art advisor to private and institutional art collectors and a dealer in modern and contemporary art. His Soho gallery, Deitch Projects, was established in 1996 and closed in 2010.

Henry Geldzahler (1935-1994) was a curator, art historian, and public arts official. Originally a curator at The Metropolitan Museum of Art, where he organized the groundbreaking 1969 exhibition, *New York Painting and Sculpture: 1940-1970*, Geldzahler later served as the first director of the Visual Arts program at the National Endowment for the Arts, and as Commissioner of Cultural Affairs in New York City from 1977 to 1982.

Carlo McCormick is senior editor of *Paper* magazine. He has authored numerous books, monographs and catalogues on contemporary art and artists, and his writing has appeared in in *Aperture*, *Art in America*, *Art News*, *Artforum*, and other magazines. He was curator (in consultation with Lynn Gumpert and Marvin J. Taylor) of *The Downtown Show: the New York Art Scene from 1974 to 1984*, which debuted at the Grey Art Gallery and Fales Library at NYU in 2006 before traveling to the Andy Warhol Museum in Pittsburgh.

Larry Warsh has been active in the art world for more than thirty years as a publisher and artist-collaborator. An early collector of Keith Haring and Jean-Michel Basquiat, Warsh was a lead organizer for the exhibition *Basquiat: The Unknown Notebooks,* which debuted at the Brooklyn Museum, New York, in 2015, and later travelled to several American museums. He has been involved in numerous exhibitions worldwide, and he served as a curatorial consultant on *Keith Haring | Jean-Michel Basquiat: Crossing Lines* for the NGV. The founder of Museums Magazine, Warsh has been involved in many publishing projects and is the editor of several other titles published by Princeton University Press, including *Haring-isms* (2020), *Basquiat-isms* (2019), *Jean-Michel Basquiat: The Notebooks* (2017), *Futura-isms* (2021), *Abloh-isms* (2021), *Arsham-isms* (2021), and *Weiwei-isms* (2012). Warsh has served on the board of the Getty Museum Photographs Council, and was a founding member of the Basquiat Authentication Committee until it's dissolution in 2012.

No More Rulers (NMR) is a platform representing empowerment, respect, and breaking down the barriers of the art world. NMR partners with leading international institutions, legacy artists and estates to validate creators through channels of connection, exhibition, and distribution. By connecting audiences with narratives from both top creators and new voices, NMR hopes to empower the creative community and help both the community and establishments to rethink the status quo..

~~NO MORE RULERS~~

Acknowledgements

This book would not have been possible without the participation and support of many individuals.

Heartfelt thanks to:

Hannah Alderfer	Carlo McCormick
Patrick Amsellem	Metropolitan Transportation Authority
Barry Blinderman	Hiroko Onoda
Tricia Laughlin Bloom	Raphaela Platow
Jeffrey Deitch	Jeffrey Posternak
Susan Delson	Annelise Ream
Janet and Jonathan Geldzahler	Tony Shafrazi
Julia Gruen	David Stark
George Horner	Taliesin Thomas
Arnold Lehman	Gil Vasquez

In Memoriam

Keith Haring
Allan Arnold
Bobby Breslau
Arch Connelly
Henry Geldzahler
Kiely Jenkins
Rene Ricard
Michael Stewart
Tseng Kwong Chi
David Wojnarowicz
O.W.

Photo Credits: Pages 12-13, 20-21, 26 (top), 28, 44-45, 52, 53, 60: Tseng Kwong Chi. Pages 10-11: Hima Selim. Page 16: unknown. Page 26 (bottom): Ivan Dalla Tana. Page 36: Elinor Vernhes. Page 37: Klaus Wittman. Page 67: Keith Haring. *Self portrait Polaroid.* $4^{1}/_{4}$ x $3^{1}/_{4}$. (10.8 x 5.25cm). Courtesy of the Keith Haring Foundation, Inc.

Photographs by Tseng Kwong Chi © Muna Tseng Dance Projects, Inc., New York.

Designed by Hannah Alderfer, HHA Design
Edited by Susan Delson
Limited edition of 3,000 copies

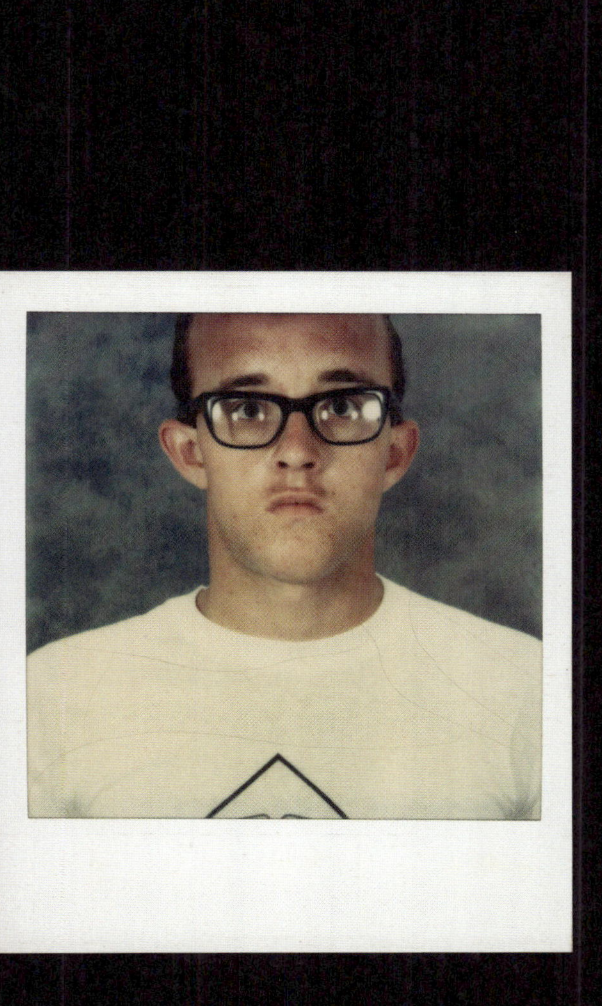